TRY THESE—FROM **CLAIRE'S** CORNUCOPIA OF VEGETARIAN DELIGHTS

Cheddar Scones Delicious served at breakfast with apple butter, at lunch with curried egg salad and a little mango chutney, or at dinner with a salad, these big, cheesy scones are so good you'll make them every weekend!

Mushrooms Fra Diavolo This devilishly good sauce, redolent of red wine, garlic, tomatoes, and mushrooms, is served over linguine. Use bread to soak up any that remains on the plate— it's too good to waste!

Vegetable Bean with Barley Soup The first soup made at Claire's, it's thick with chunks of carrots, celery, and potatoes and subtly flavored with spices—a healthy whole-meal soup that's a perennial favorite at the Corner Copia, and will be at your house too!

Deep Dish Gourmet Pizza A savory batter bread baked with vegetables, cheese, and marinara sauce, this is a house specialty made even more versatile by using low-fat ricotta cheese in the middle of this aromatic "pizza."

Lithuanian Coffee Cake The most popular cake at **Claire's**, with a unique coffee, walnut, and raisin filling, it smells and tastes incredibly delicious.

CLAIRE CRISCUOLO founded **Claire's Corner Copia** in 1975, on the same New Haven corner where it stands today. She and her restaurant have won numerous awards for cooking and community activism, and in 1993 she received the award for Outstanding Community Service from AIDS Project/ New Haven. She lives in New Haven, Connecticut.

Claire's Corner Copia Cookbook

225 Homestyle Vegetarian Recipes from **Claire's** Family to Yours

Claire Criscuolo

A PLUME BOOK

PLUME
Published by the Penguin Group
Penguin Books USA Inc., 375 Hudson Street,
New York, New York 10014, U.S.A.
Penguin Books Ltd, 27 Wrights Lane,
London W8 5TZ, England
Penguin Books Australia Ltd, Ringwood,
Victoria, Australia
Penguin Books Canada Ltd, 10 Alcorn Avenue,
Toronto, Ontario, Canada M4V 3B2
Penguin Books (N.Z.) Ltd, 182–190 Wairau Road,
Auckland 10, New Zealand

Penguin Books Ltd, Registered Offices:
Harmondsworth, Middlesex, England

First published by Plume, an imprint of Dutton Signet, a division of Penguin Books USA
Inc.

First Printing, November, 1994

10 9 8 7 6 5 4 3 2 1

 REGISTERED TRADEMARK—MARCA REGISTRADA

LIBRARY OF CONGRESS CATALOGING IN PUBLICATION DATA:

Criscuolo, Claire.
    Claire's Corner Copia cookbook : 225 homestyle vegetarian recipes
from Claire's family to yours / by Claire Criscuolo.
        p.   cm.
    ISBN 0-452-27176-2
    1. Vegetarian cookery. 2. Claire's Corner Copia (Restaurant)
I. Title.
TX837.C77 1994
641.5′636—dc20   94-11882
                                                                        CIP

Printed in the United States of America
Set in Sabon
Designed by Leonard Telesca

BOOKS ARE AVAILABLE AT QUANTITY DISCOUNTS WHEN USED TO PROMOTE PRODUCTS OR SERVICES.
FOR INFORMATION PLEASE WRITE TO PREMIUM MARKETING DIVISION, PENGUIN BOOKS USA INC.,
375 HUDSON STREET, NEW YORK, NEW YORK 10014.

This book is
lovingly dedicated to my mother, Anna,
and to my husband, Frank.

Acknowledgments

Behind every successful business is a caring and talented staff. I will always be grateful for the many hardworking, bright, and energetic employees who helped make **Claire's** the success it is. I am especially grateful to Sara Sylvester, Sally Tessler, Harriet Dichter, Wendy Read, David Peck, Jim Morotti, Jenny Humphry, Donna Nuzzello, Rebeccah Pugh, Becky Seashore, Erika Zucker, Lynne Agustinelli, Pat McCardle, Tom Albin, Jim Carter, Zeke Barrera, Kyomi Chiba, Kirsten Kvist-Hansen, Vanessa Oliver, Javier Lopez, Laurie Savastano, Karis Wold, Teddy and Tama Monoson, Pilar and Eben Stewart, Armando Velasquez, the crew from S.A.R.A.H., Kauaneekee Hernandez, Bill Karpell, Doug Gavoli, Kerry Tesoriero, and Nicanor Lucero. Anita Lawrence and Rose Naclerio-Albin played a major role in our success during their many years at **Claire's**. Chrissy Savastano has worked at **Claire's** since 1986 and I couldn't have left **Claire's** in better hands when I left to write this book. Don Jackson has been an amazing line cook, manager, and muffin maker at **Claire's** for nine years. Our customers are the best any business could ask for. Thank you for your loyal support, and for all the helpful suggestions you've given to us over the years.

I couldn't have written this book without the encouragement of my husband, Frank, the ideas and recipes from my mom, the constant help of my mother- and father-in-law, the love from my family and friends, and the months of taste testing by Sara and Walter Johnson. My friends Phyllis Monoson, Claudia Marrone, and Lynda Stewart were a tremendous help whenever I thought I couldn't write another word. Julia Moskin convinced Penguin USA to publish this book and then she and Rena Kornbluh made it better by editing it. I am grateful to them and to my agent, Carole Abel, for believing in this book.

My thanks would not be complete without offering praise to God.

Contents

Introduction

This is a cookbook of the foods we serve at our vegetarian restaurant, Claire's Corner Copia in New Haven, Connecticut. I founded **Claire's** with my husband, Frank, in 1975; I was twenty-four and full of energy, and I believed eating habits were changing. Most people said I was crazy. At that time, vegetarians were considered weird or at least unusual; Mollie Katzen's Moosewood Restaurant in Ithaca, New York, was only three years old, and people thought vegetarianism was a fad. Well, with the help of my family and my staff, **Claire's** became a bustling fixture in downtown New Haven; nineteen years later, we're still going strong.

I've lived in New Haven all my life. I grew up on Wooster Street, where many immigrants from Amalfi in Southern Italy came to live in the early 1900s. It was and is a thriving Italian-American community, with pastry shops, grocery stores (including my grandfather's shop, which was known as Paolo's), and of course pizza parlors. Pepe's and Sally's famous pizzerias were right down the street. My mother also grew up in the Wooster Street area, and while her brothers were helping my grandfather at the store, she was learning to cook from her mother, my Grandmother Assunta. She always had a pot of soup going on the stove—and my mother carried on her tradition. When I was younger, I didn't always appreciate my mother's dedication to cooking. I thought she spent too much time in the kitchen, and wished I could have the canned ravioli and packaged desserts my friends enjoyed. In fact, when she first tried to teach me how to cook, I looked her in the face and said, "Don't waste your time, Mom. I have no intention of making housewifery a career." Now cooking is my livelihood

and my love, and I've eaten my words along with hundreds of delicious dishes she and I have cooked together.

My mother always cooked healthful foods for us, although when I was growing up in the 1950s with my three brothers, there wasn't as much nutritional research to back up her beliefs as there is now. She wasn't a scientific pioneer; she was just cooking from a family tradition she believed in. She always said, "If I can't pronounce an ingredient on the label, it doesn't belong in my stomach." She stayed away from foods with additives, and her eye was so well trained that she could tell freshness and ripeness at a glance. Her idea of convenience food was a tin of peeled imported tomatoes for her marinara sauce. We ate lots of beans, lentils, rice, and pasta and only the freshest vegetables and fruits, and even had freshly squeezed orange juice every morning. I was so thoroughly spoiled by Mom's cooking that my first meal in a college dining hall was quite a shock. The canned tomato soup wasn't anything like the deeply flavored combination of fresh tomatoes, fresh herbs, and olive oil I knew by that name. The limp cold cuts they called lunch didn't begin to compare to the lunches Mom had always packed for me, with her peppers and eggs, zucchini parmigiana, and even lasagna in a thermos.

When my husband and I decided to go into business together, we knew a restaurant was the perfect choice. I saw that the women of my generation didn't have the time for cooking that their mothers had, and I knew from my own experience that hungry college students sorely miss home-cooked meals. Since Frank and I both had deep roots in New Haven, Yale University was the obvious location—and still is. We found and renovated a bright, airy corner space with large windows, exposed brick walls, and a gorgeous view of the New Haven Green and the Yale campus. I built a kitchen from scratch. The previous tenant had been a popcorn store, so I sold their caramel-popcorn-making equipment and bought a four-burner stove. I turned their display case into a salad bar. Our families donated their extra kitchenware, and I called my mom and asked, "What should the first soup be?"

The first soup turned out to be Vegetable Bean Soup with Barley, served with homemade honey wheat bread, which I kneaded by hand. From there, our menu expanded rapidly. Soups are still the cornerstone of the menu, but our muffins, cakes, crisps, and cookies are a close second in popularity. In everything we cook, we take advantage of the freshest ingredients, the glorious bounty of each season. The tender first asparagus of spring becomes part of a delicate quiche or

frittata. We celebrate the locally grown produce of our summers by using those splendid, perfectly ripened tomatoes in panzanella, fresh tomato sauces, and pasta salads. Bagfuls of summer basil become delicious pestos; sweet berries fill our muffins and cobblers. Fall and winter bring the delightful aromas and flavors of acorn squash with savory fillings, roasted sweet potatoes with chickpeas, and luscious apple and pumpkin pies. When we introduced Middle Eastern foods like falafel, hummus, and tabouli, and Mexican specialties like burritos, Eggplant Veracruz, and enchiladas, these foods were new to many of our customers, especially in vegetarian versions. Now they're on menus everywhere.

Americans' eating habits have changed a lot since 1975. In fact, when **Claire's** first opened, it wasn't completely vegetarian. But Frances Moore Lappé's *Diet for a Small Planet* made so much sense to us that by 1977 we had banned meat and poultry from the menu (and banned smoking from the restaurant). Today's nutritional research continues to support those decisions. The fresh fruits and vegetables, hearty grains and beans, and low-fat pastas and breads we serve at **Claire's** are now recognized as the building blocks of a nutritious diet. We use yogurt, low-fat milk, and low-fat sour cream whenever possible, but I've never found an adequate substitute for butter in favorite desserts like Lithuanian Coffee Cake and Chocolate Cake. The bottom line for all the food at **Claire's** is taste; if the dishes we offer are healthful but not delicious, no one will eat them, so they are both. We believe—along with the many health professionals from nearby Yale/New Haven Hospital who eat at **Claire's** every day—that there is room in even the healthiest diet for occasional indulgences like dessert or a cream soup.

Over the years at **Claire's,** we've changed the food, but never our philosophy. We treat everything and everyone with respect, from our ingredients to our employees and the many people whose lives are connected with the restaurant. When we opened, our full-time staff consisted of Frank and me and our families. Our first paid employee didn't start until 1977; now many of our staff, from dishwashers to managers, have been with us for years, and they truly are part of the **Claire's** family. Thanks to the support the New Haven community has given us from the beginning, we've been able to give something back by participating in local programs like Rachel's Table, Share Our Strength, and AIDS Project/New Haven.

Today we have thirty-five employees, a ten-burner stove, and a huge crowd

of regulars. My mom still runs the kitchen three days a week; Frank's dad bakes our famous breads; Frank's mom cooks her amazing manicotti, and all our brothers, sisters, in-laws, and their kids are our permanent best tasters. The **Claire's** family gets bigger all the time. I feel privileged to make an honest living at something I love to do; while it hasn't always been easy, I would do it again, in a heartbeat.

Claire Criscuolo
New Haven, Connecticut
May 1994

Breakfast

Breakfast has regained its popularity, and I couldn't be happier. It's my favorite meal to eat, make, or serve. Many of us are too busy to make a cooked breakfast every day, but most of these recipes allow for a busy schedule. You can prepare a muffin or scone batter at night and bake it in the morning. Granola for the whole week can be made on Sunday: it will keep for days and you can decide exactly what goes in it. Breakfast Pudding and Breakfast Baked Apples can be made in advance and reheated. Shakes are perfect for those of us who are chronically running late. And you can enjoy wonderful pancakes on your treasured mornings off.

Maple-Nut Granola

SERVES 8

Pure maple syrup gives this granola its delicious flavor. Please don't be tempted by imitation maple syrup. It's not even close in flavor or contents.

  6 cups rolled oats
  ½ cup chopped walnuts
  ½ cup sliced almonds
  ¼ cup wheat germ
  2 teaspoons cinnamon
  1 cup pure maple syrup
  2 tablespoons soybean or vegetable oil
  ½ cup chopped dried figs
  ½ cup chopped dried apple rings

Preheat the oven to 250 degrees. In a bowl, combine the oats, walnuts, almonds, wheat germ, and cinnamon. In another bowl, whisk together the maple syrup and oil; pour this mixture over the oat mixture all at once. Toss well.

Spread evenly in a shallow baking dish or on a cookie sheet. Bake for 1½ hours, stirring every 15 minutes.

Stir in the figs and apples. Continue baking about 30 minutes, until the mixture feels dry. Cool to room temperature. Store in a covered container at room temperature, up to 1 week.

Honey-Sweetened Granola

SERVES 8

This easy-to-prepare breakfast cereal will make you forget store-bought. Enjoy it with a sliced banana and milk, or sprinkle some on yogurt. I like to double or triple the recipe and fill mason jars for gifts.

   6 cups rolled oats
   ¼ cup sunflower seeds
   ¼ cup chopped walnuts
   ¼ cup wheat germ
   2 teaspoons cinnamon
   ½ cup apple juice, fresh-pressed or unfiltered
   2 tablespoons canola oil
   1 tablespoon vanilla extract
   ½ cup honey
   ½ cup raisins

Preheat the oven to 250 degrees. In a bowl, toss together the oats, sunflower seeds, walnuts, wheat germ, and cinnamon. In a separate bowl, whisk together the apple juice, oil, vanilla extract, and honey; pour this over the oat mixture and toss to coat evenly.

Turn the granola into a rectangular glass baking dish, spreading it evenly. Bake uncovered about 2 hours, stirring every 15 minutes, until the mixture is dry. Stir in the raisins. Cool to room temperature, then store in a tightly covered container at room temperature, up to 1 week.

Cheddar Scones

MAKES 6 LARGE SCONES

Cheddar scones are delicious served at breakfast with apple butter; they make a wonderful lunch sandwich when filled with curried egg salad and a little mango chutney; and they are the perfect accompaniment to a salad with dinner. We shape our scones to the size of a tennis ball before baking—they come out huge, and our customers love them. My friend Phyllis and my brother Paul drive out of their way just for these scones.

> 1¾ cups flour
> 2 teaspoons baking powder
> 1 tablespoon sugar
> ½ teaspoon salt
> ½ cup grated cheddar
> 4 tablespoons (½ stick) butter, cut into ½-inch cubes
> 2 eggs, lightly beaten
> ⅓ cup buttermilk or sour milk

Preheat the oven to 375 degrees. In a large bowl, sift together the flour, baking powder, sugar, and salt. Add the cheddar and stir to mix well. Add the butter and rub into the flour mixture with your fingers until it resembles coarse cornmeal.

In a separate bowl, whisk together the eggs and buttermilk or sour milk about 30 seconds. Pour the liquid over the flour mixture all at once and stir with a spoon until just combined. The dough should be fairly stiff.

Drop 6 big spoonfuls of batter onto a cookie sheet that is nonstick or has been lined with parchment paper. Leave as much space as possible in between for spreading. Centering the cookie sheet on the middle oven rack, bake about 30 minutes, until the scones are golden brown and a tester inserted into the center of each comes out clean.

Chocolate-Chip and Wheat Scones

MAKES 8 LARGE SCONES

We bake these scones at **Claire's** for breakfast, but you can also enjoy them mid-morning with coffee for a break from work or studies. The scones are good plain or with raspberry jam.

  2 cups unbleached flour
  1 cup whole-wheat flour
  ¼ cup sugar
  4 teaspoons baking powder
  ¼ teaspoon salt
  2 tablespoons freshly grated orange zest
 12 tablespoons (1½ sticks) butter, cut into 12 pieces
  1 egg, lightly beaten
  1 cup buttermilk or sour milk
  ½ teaspoon vanilla extract
  ½ cup chocolate chips
  ¼ cup chopped walnuts

Preheat the oven to 375 degrees. In a bowl, sift together the unbleached flour, whole-wheat flour, sugar, baking powder, and salt. Stir in the orange zest. Using 2 knives, cut the butter into the flour mixture until it resembles coarse crumbs.

In a separate bowl, whisk together the egg, buttermilk or sour milk, and vanilla extract. Pour the liquid over the flour mixture all at once and stir just to combine. Stir in the chocolate chips and walnuts.

Line a cookie sheet with parchment paper or grease lightly. Drop the scone batter by 8 heaping spoonfuls onto the cookie sheet, leaving as much space in between as possible to allow for spreading. Bake for 40 minutes on the center rack of the oven. The scones are done when a cake tester inserted into the center of each comes out clean.

Breakfast Pudding

SERVES 8

I enjoyed a variety of homemade puddings while growing up. My mom cooked breakfast puddings and chocolate, vanilla, or lemon pudding as fillings for her cream puffs and sponge cakes. I still can't resist an occasional homemade pudding. This is an updated version of Mom's breakfast pudding. I have replaced the whole eggs with egg substitute and the cream and whole milk with soy milk. It's different, but still rich, delicious, and an excellent choice for breakfast. This pudding is convenient too; you can bake it in advance and enjoy it for up to three days.

> One 16-ounce carton egg substitute
> Two 28-ounce boxes soy milk (found in the health-food section of many
>   supermarkets)
> ¼ cup wheat germ
> 2½ teaspoons cinnamon
> ½ teaspoon nutmeg
> ½ cup blackstrap molasses
> 2 apples, thinly sliced
> 2 bananas, thinly sliced
> 4 apricots, fresh or dried, pitted and chopped
> 6 big slices whole-wheat bread, torn into pieces

Preheat the oven to 375 degrees. In a bowl, whisk together the egg substitute, soy milk, wheat germ, 2 teaspoons of the cinnamon, the nutmeg, and molasses for 1 minute. Stir in the apples, bananas, apricots, and bread.

Spray a rectangular glass baking dish with nonstick cooking spray. Pour the mixture into the prepared dish and let stand for 15 minutes to allow the bread to absorb the liquid. Sprinkle the remaining ½ teaspoon cinnamon over the top. Bake for 1½ hours, until the center is set.

Gingerbread-Apple Pancakes

SERVES 4

These are lovely muffin-like pancakes, great with warm maple syrup or lemon yogurt.

  3 cups whole-wheat flour
  4 teaspoons baking powder
  2 teaspoons cinnamon
  1 teaspoon allspice
  3 eggs, lightly beaten
  1½ cups low-fat milk
  ½ cup plus 1 tablespoon blackstrap molasses
  1 teaspoon vanilla extract
  1 tablespoon soybean or vegetable oil
  2 tablespoons unsweetened applesauce
  1 small apple, peeled, grated, and drained (by pressing in a colander)
  1 teaspoon freshly grated orange zest

In a bowl, whisk together the flour, baking powder, cinnamon, and allspice. In another bowl, whisk together the remaining ingredients. Pour the liquid over the flour mixture and stir until thoroughly combined.

Heat a nonstick griddle or skillet over low heat. Spoon on 1 heaping tablespoon batter per pancake. Cook about 10 minutes, until the bottom is browned and somewhat firm. Using a plastic spatula, flip carefully. Lightly press the pancake to flatten it slightly. Cook for another 5 to 10 minutes, until done.

Oatmeal Pancakes

SERVES 4

We always serve our oatmeal pancakes with fresh fruit and pure maple syrup. During the summer months we use finely diced, perfectly ripened peaches or beautiful, plump blueberries, and in fall and winter we add finely diced, crisp apples or pears. In between, we slip slices of ripe banana into the batter, or sauté banana slices in a little butter and serve them on top of these beautiful pancakes.

- 2 cups rolled oats
- 1¾ cups buttermilk
- ¼ cup freshly squeezed orange juice
- 2 eggs, lightly beaten
- 4 tablespoons (½ stick) butter or soy margarine, melted (soy margarine can be found in health-food stores)
- ½ cup unbleached flour
- 1 tablespoon sugar
- 2 teaspoons freshly grated orange zest
- 1 teaspoon baking powder
- 1 teaspoon baking soda
- ¼ teaspoon cinnamon
  Pinch nutmeg
  Pinch salt
- 1 cup finely diced peaches, apples, pears, strawberries, or blueberries
  Walnut oil for brushing the griddle

In a large bowl, combine the oats, buttermilk, and orange juice. Set aside for 15 minutes. Add the eggs and melted butter or margarine and beat about 30 seconds to combine well. Add the flour, sugar, orange zest, baking powder, baking soda, cinnamon, nutmeg, and salt; stir to mix well. Gently fold in the fruit.

Heat a nonstick griddle or skillet over medium heat. Brush lightly with walnut oil. Pour the batter in ¼ cupfuls onto the heated griddle, leaving space in between for turning. Cook until golden brown, about 2 minutes, then flip gently with a plastic spatula. Cook the other side until golden brown, about 2 minutes.

Corn-Walnut Muffins

MAKES 1 DOZEN MUFFINS

Don Jackson is our treasured line cook. He has made many delicious foods for us at **Claire's,** and these are his favorite muffins. Bake a batch and freeze any leftovers. You can defrost them in your microwave or in the oven as you need them.

    2 cups unbleached flour
    2 cups yellow cornmeal
    ⅓ cup sugar
    2 tablespoons baking powder
    1 teaspoon salt
    4 eggs
    2 cups milk
    ¼ cup soybean or vegetable oil
    ¼ cup unsweetened applesauce
        Freshly grated zest of 1 orange
    ⅓ cup chopped walnuts

Preheat the oven to 375 degrees. In a large bowl, whisk together the flour, cornmeal, sugar, baking powder, and salt. In a separate bowl, whisk the eggs lightly. Whisk in the milk, oil, applesauce, and zest. Pour the liquid ingredients over the dry ingredients all at once. Mix with a spoon just until thoroughly combined. (Don't beat the batter or it will produce tough muffins.) Stir in the walnuts.

Spray a muffin tin with nonstick cooking spray, or grease and flour each cup. Fill each cup two-thirds full. Bake for 25 to 30 minutes, until a tester inserted in the center comes out clean. Let stand for 5 minutes before turning out.

Oatmeal-Raisin Muffins

MAKES 1 DOZEN MUFFINS

This is a tasty way to increase your consumption of fiber. During raspberry season, we substitute fresh raspberries for the raisins.

    2 cups unbleached flour
    2 cups rolled oats
    4 teaspoons baking powder
    ½ teaspoon baking soda
    ½ teaspoon salt
    ½ cup firmly packed brown sugar
    ½ teaspoon nutmeg
    1 teaspoon cinnamon
      Freshly grated zest of 1 lemon
    2 eggs
  1½ cups buttermilk
    ½ cup soybean or vegetable oil
    ¼ cup unsweetened applesauce

Preheat the oven to 375 degrees. In a large bowl, whisk together the flour, oats, baking powder, baking soda, salt, sugar, nutmeg, cinnamon, and zest. In a separate bowl, lightly whisk the eggs. Whisk in the buttermilk, oil, and applesauce. Pour the liquid ingredients over the dry all at once and stir together just until all the flour is blended in. (Do not beat, or the muffins will be tough.)

Spray a muffin tin with nonstick cooking spray, or grease and flour each cup. Fill the cups ⅔ full. Bake for 30 to 35 minutes, until a tester inserted in the center comes out clean. Let stand for 5 minutes before turning out.

Raspberry-Apple Muffins

MAKES 10 MUFFINS

We bake these for breakfast at **Claire's,** but many customers buy them to take home for a snack with their evening tea.

1½ cups flour
½ cup sugar
½ teaspoon baking soda
¼ teaspoon baking powder
¼ teaspoon salt
   Pinch nutmeg
½ teaspoon cinnamon
1 teaspoon freshly grated lemon zest
1 egg
⅓ cup milk
2 tablespoons fresh lemon juice
3 tablespoons soybean or vegetable oil
2 tablespoons unsweetened applesauce
1 cup grated apple, well drained (by pressing in a colander)
½ cup chopped walnuts
¼ cup raspberry preserves

Preheat the oven to 375 degrees. Into a large bowl, sift together the flour, sugar, baking soda, baking powder, salt, nutmeg, and cinnamon. Stir in the lemon zest. In a separate bowl, lightly whisk the egg. Add the milk, lemon juice, oil, and applesauce and whisk to combine well. Stir in the apple and pour the mixture over the dry ingredients all at once. Stir until just combined. (Do not beat, or your muffins will be tough.) Stir in the walnuts.

Spray a muffin tin with nonstick cooking spray, or grease and flour each cup. Fill the cups ⅔ full, then drop a rounded teaspoonful of preserves in the center of each. Bake about 30 minutes, or until a tester inserted into the center comes out clean. Cool in the pan for 1 minute before turning out.

Bran-Apple Muffins

MAKES 1 DOZEN MUFFINS

We make bran muffins every day at **Claire's**. Over the years, we have tried many combinations. This recipe has been a best-seller for more than eighteen years because it is rich in fiber yet moister than most bran muffins.

   2 cups bran flakes
1½ cups milk
   2 eggs
   2 tablespoons butter or soy margarine, melted (soy margarine is sold in
      most health-food stores)
¼ cup unsweetened applesauce
   2 cups unbleached flour
   4 teaspoons baking powder
½ teaspoon salt
½ cup sugar
   1 teaspoon cinnamon
      Freshly grated zest of 1 lemon
   1 large apple, peeled, cored, and finely diced

Preheat the oven to 375 degrees. Pour the bran flakes into a large bowl and pour the milk over. Let stand for 10 minutes. In a separate bowl, lightly whisk the eggs. Whisk in the melted butter or margarine and applesauce. Pour this mixture over the bran and milk mixture and stir to combine well.

In a separate bowl, stir together the flour, baking powder, salt, sugar, cinnamon, zest, and apple. Pour this mixture over the bran mixture all at once. Stir just until all the flour is mixed in. (Do not beat or the muffins will be tough.)

Spray a muffin tin with nonstick cooking spray or grease and flour each cup. Fill the cups two-thirds full. Bake for 25 to 30 minutes, until a tester inserted in the center comes out clean. Let stand for 5 minutes before turning out.

Yogurt Shake

MAKES 1 SHAKE

A yogurt shake is the healthful breakfast or lunch of choice when I'm in a hurry. We serve thousands of yogurt shakes a year at **Claire's**. This recipe and the two that follow are the most popular, but any combination of juice or milk, blended with fruit, yogurt, wheat germ, and honey, sounds good to me. Serve them right after blending or they will separate, which doesn't alter their nutritional value, but does change their appearance.

1 cup orange juice
1 large banana, broken into 3 pieces
2 tablespoons wheat germ
1 cup plain nonfat yogurt
1 tablespoon honey (optional)

Place all the ingredients in a blender. Process on high speed about 30 seconds, until blended.

Ellen's Ecstasy

MAKES 1 SHAKE

When our friend Ellen was a student at Yale, she ordered this shake every day.

1 cup milk, preferably low-fat
1 large banana, broken into 3 pieces
2 tablespoons wheat germ
1 cup plain nonfat yogurt
1 tablespoon honey

Place all the ingredients in a blender. Process on high speed about 30 seconds, until blended.

Tropical Paradise

MAKES 1 SHAKE

1 cup pineapple juice
1 cup plain nonfat yogurt
1 small banana, broken in half
1 kiwi, peeled and quartered
2 or 3 strawberries, fresh or frozen

Place all the ingredients in a blender. Process on high speed about 30 seconds, until blended.

Fresh Fruit Smoothies

MAKES 3 OR 4 SMOOTHIES

Smoothies are a popular way to enjoy two or more fruits. At home, I serve them in my favorite wine glasses. Children will enjoy being included when you're relaxing with these "cocktails."

2½ cups pineapple juice
2 ice cubes
8 to 10 strawberries, fresh or frozen
2 tablespoons wheat germ

or:

2½ cups grapefruit juice
2 ice cubes
3 kiwi, peeled and quartered
2 tablespoons wheat germ

Place all the ingredients in a blender. Process on high speed about 30 seconds, until blended. Serve immediately, or reblend for 5 seconds just before serving.

Breakfast Baked Apples

SERVES 6

We enjoy these baked apples any time of day. They're rich-tasting with or without the butter.

   6 large baking apples (Rome or McIntosh are our favorites)
   2 cups apple cider (fresh-pressed, if possible)
      Cinnamon for sprinkling
   4 tablespoons (½ stick) butter, cut into 6 pats (optional)
   2 teaspoons vanilla extract

Topping:

   3 cups plain nonfat yogurt
   2 tablespoons honey
   1 teaspoon cinnamon

Preheat the oven to 425 degrees. Cut a 1-inch top off each apple, and core the apples. Arrange the apples cut side up in a glass baking pan 2 or 3 inches deep and large enough to hold the apples in a single layer. Pour the cider over the apples. Sprinkle each apple with cinnamon. If desired, top each apple with a pat of butter. Pour ¼ teaspoon vanilla extract on top of each apple and pour the remaining ½ teaspoon into the cider in the pan. Cover tightly with foil.

Bake for 30 minutes, then uncover and baste. Replace the foil and continue baking for 15 to 30 minutes, until cooked to the desired softness.

Combine the topping ingredients, transfer the apples to individual bowls, and divide the topping among the bowls.

French (Italian) Toast

SERVES 4

My mom has always had a knack for turning leftovers into marvelous new meals. This delicious French toast is made with leftover Italian bread. During the week, our day-old Italian bread was used for stuffing peppers, zucchini, or eggplant or for making garlic croutons or bread pudding, but the Italian bread left over from Saturday was used for this special French toast, and my brothers and I always looked forward to it. Although I mainly eat whole-grain breads today, I sometimes buy a loaf of Italian bread on Saturday and save it for the next day, just to make this wonderful French toast. I serve it with pure maple syrup and applesauce, or top it with lightly sautéed slices of banana.

> 4 eggs, lightly beaten
> 3 tablespoons low-fat milk or soy milk
> ½ teaspoon cinnamon
> ½ teaspoon vanilla extract
>   Pinch nutmeg
> Eight 1-inch slices day-old Italian bread
> 1 tablespoon butter or soy margarine (soy margarine can be found in
>   health-food stores)

In a large bowl, whisk together the eggs, milk, cinnamon, vanilla extract, and nutmeg. Add the slices of bread, and completely coat each slice. Let soak for 10 minutes.

Melt the butter in a large nonstick skillet over medium-low heat. Using a fork, lift out the slices of bread 1 at a time and arrange them in the skillet. Cook for 2 or 3 minutes, until golden brown. Using a plastic spatula, turn and cook the other side until golden brown.

Soups

Hearty soups have always been a staple at **Claire's**. From our first four-quart soup pot in 1975 to the twenty- and forty-quart pots we now use, we sell gallons of soups with our homemade bread every day, whether the temperature is two degrees or ninety-two. Once again, I must thank my mom for introducing soups into my diet. She is the greatest soup maker I know.

With most of our soups, a cupful can be a perfect start to a meal. A bowlful can be almost a meal in itself; add some good bread and a salad and you may not want more.

We use dried beans for our soups. We cook them for two or three hours so that the beans have plenty of time to soften properly and thicken the soup. Chickpeas sometimes take longer to cook, so we often soak them overnight in water in the refrigerator, then drain, rinse, and proceed with the recipe. These soups freeze well. Label and date each container and store it for up to one month. You might want to make two or three soups at the same time and freeze for future meals, or you can give your friends and family lovely gifts of soup. My mom still sends my brothers home each week with a container of her soup. With their busy schedules, they appreciate this treat.

Once you get in the habit of preparing fresh soups, you will never again settle for canned, and you won't have to.

Cuban Black Bean Soup

SERVES 8

Serve this filling soup with a sprinkling of finely chopped red onion.

     4½ quarts water
    12 ounces black beans, picked over
     ½ cup plus 1 tablespoon olive oil
    10 cloves garlic, minced
     ½ teaspoon crushed red pepper flakes
     ½ teaspoon fennel seeds
     1 bay leaf
     1 cup chopped parsley
   One 28-ounce can whole tomatoes in juice, crushed with your hands
     ½ cup brown rice, uncooked
       Salt to taste
     1 teaspoon black pepper

Bring the water to a boil in a large covered pot. Add the beans, olive oil, garlic, red pepper flakes, fennel seeds, bay leaf, and parsley. Cook over medium heat, uncovered, for 1 hour, stirring frequently. Add the tomatoes and continue cooking for 30 minutes. Add the rice, salt, and pepper. Lower the heat and simmer for 1 hour, stirring frequently, until the beans are very soft. Taste for seasoning.

Escarole and Bean Soup

SERVES 8

Escarole can be found in the produce section of most supermarkets. The entire head (minus the stem) is delicious in soups. The tender, pale green inner leaves also make a delicious salad.

     4 quarts water
    12 ounces great northern beans, picked over
     8 large cloves garlic, minced
    ½ small head green cabbage, chopped
     1 cup chopped parsley
     1 teaspoon fennel seeds
    ½ teaspoon crushed red pepper flakes
    10 leaves fresh basil, chopped, or ½ teaspoon dried basil
    ½ cup plus 1 tablespoon olive oil
     2 medium potatoes, diced
     1 teaspoon black pepper
     2 large heads escarole, chopped
       Salt to taste

Bring the water to a boil in a large covered pot. Add the beans, garlic, cabbage, parsley, fennel seeds, red pepper flakes, basil, and olive oil. Return to a boil, then lower the heat to medium and cook, uncovered, for 1½ hours, stirring every 5 to 10 minutes. Add the potatoes, pepper, escarole, and salt. Continue cooking over medium-low heat for 1 hour, stirring frequently, until the beans are soft and the broth is creamy. Taste for seasoning.

Split Pea Soup

SERVES 6

I love split pea soup. Mom always made delectable variations of it when my brothers and I lived at home. She still comes up with new vegetable combinations, and we try them on our willing customers at **Claire's.** She hasn't disappointed them yet. This is a popular version, but also try replacing the spinach with chopped carrots and celery, the barley with brown rice, and the white potatoes with sweet potatoes. Split peas are soft and will stick to the bottom of your soup pot and burn if you are not careful. Stir the soup often and lower the heat if you notice it's beginning to stick.

      4 quarts water
      1 pound split peas (green or yellow), picked over
      2 small onions, chopped
      8 tablespoons (1 stick) butter or margarine
      2 cloves garlic, chopped
      ¼ cup chopped flat-leaf parsley
      ½ teaspoon dried basil
      ¼ pound barley
      1 bay leaf
      4 large potatoes, diced
   One 10-ounce bag fresh spinach, rinsed and chopped
         Salt to taste
      1 teaspoon black pepper

Bring the water to a boil in a large covered pot. Add the split peas, onions, butter, garlic, parsley, basil, barley, and bay leaf. Lower the heat and cook uncovered over low heat, stirring frequently, for 45 minutes. Add the potatoes and spinach. Continue cooking over low heat for 45 minutes to 1 hour, stirring frequently. Stir in the salt and pepper. Taste for seasoning.

Creamy Pea Soup with Rice and Mint

SERVES 6 TO 8

This soup is both good to eat and good to look at. I love the combination of split and whole green peas with rice and mint. The soup is rich, so we make it only a few times a year.

    3 quarts water
    1 pound split peas, picked over
    2 small onions, chopped
    2 cloves garlic, chopped
    5 medium carrots, diced
    ½ bunch celery, diced
    ¼ cup chopped parsley
    4 tablespoons (½ stick) butter
    ½ cup brown rice, uncooked
    1 teaspoon dried mint
One 10-ounce box frozen green peas
    2 cups (1 pint) heavy cream
    3 cups milk
      Salt to taste
    1 teaspoon black pepper

Bring the water to a boil in a large covered pot. Add the split peas, onions, garlic, carrots, celery, parsley, butter, rice, and mint. Lower the heat and cook uncovered, stirring frequently, for 1¼ hours, until the rice is cooked and the soup is thick. Add the frozen peas and continue cooking for another 15 minutes, stirring frequently. Stir in the cream, milk, salt, and pepper. Cook, stirring constantly, for 2 minutes, until heated through. Taste for seasoning.

Vegetable Bean Soup with Barley

SERVES 8

This is the first soup I sold at **Claire's,** back in 1975. I made it in an 8-quart pot on the range given to me by my husband's grandmother, and our customers loved it right away. We continue to serve this healthful whole-meal soup today, only we now cook it in 22-quart pots during the warm months and 40-quart pots during the winter months.

        4 quarts water
        ½ pound kidney beans, picked over
        ½ pound great northern beans, picked over
        1 cup olive oil
        6 cloves garlic
        ¼ cup chopped flat-leaf parsley
        2 small onions, chopped
        ¼ pound barley
        6 carrots, chopped
        ½ bunch celery, chopped
        ½ teaspoon dried basil
        ½ teaspoon dried oregano
        1 bay leaf
One 28-ounce can whole tomatoes, crushed with your hands
        2 large potatoes, diced
        ½ 10-ounce bag fresh spinach, rinsed and chopped
            Salt to taste
        1 teaspoon black pepper

Bring the water to a boil in a large covered pot. Stir in the kidney beans and cook uncovered over medium heat for 50 minutes, stirring occasionally. Add the great northern beans, olive oil, garlic, parsley, onions, and barley. Cook, stirring frequently, over medium heat for 30 minutes. Add the carrots, celery, basil, oregano, bay leaf, and tomatoes. Cook over medium heat, stirring frequently, for 1 hour, or until the beans are tender. Add the potatoes, spinach, salt, and pepper. Continue cooking, stirring frequently, for 30 minutes. Test for seasoning.

Lentil Vegetable Soup

SERVES 8

We always thought of our lentil soup as simple and unpretentious—that is, until it was requested for the luncheon we catered for our local ABC station when the network executives came to town. It was a big hit. Now we know it's a fine choice for any occasion.

    4 quarts water
    6 cloves garlic, minced
   12 ounces lentils, picked over
    ½ cup barley
    ½ cup olive oil
    1 bunch celery, chopped
    5 medium carrots, chopped
    1 cup chopped parsley
    1 medium yellow onion, chopped
    ¼ teaspoon dried basil or 2 tablespoons chopped fresh basil
    2 potatoes, diced
      Salt to taste
    1 teaspoon black pepper

Bring the water to a boil in a large covered pot. Add the garlic, lentils, barley, olive oil, celery, carrots, parsley, onion, and basil. Bring to a boil, lower the heat, and simmer for 1¼ hours, stirring frequently. Add the potatoes, salt, and pepper and continue cooking for 30 minutes, stirring frequently, until the lentils are very soft and the soup is thick. Taste for seasoning.

Curried Lentil Soup

SERVES 6

One day back in the late 1970s, a customer asked if we would prepare a lentil soup flavored with curry. We started out with a mild curry flavor, and over the years we have developed this recipe, which has a little more spice than the original. We also put in brown rice, which gives it a nice nuttiness. We sometimes add chopped potatoes and broccoli during the last 30 minutes of cooking.

      ½ cup olive oil
      3 cloves garlic, chopped
      3 large onions, chopped
      1 tablespoon curry powder
      ⅛ teaspoon cayenne pepper
      1 bay leaf
      ¼ cup chopped flat-leaf parsley
      4 quarts water
      1 pound lentils, picked over
      ½ cup brown rice, uncooked
  One 10-ounce box frozen peas
      ¼ cup bottled mango chutney (found in the condiment section of most
         supermarkets)
         Salt to taste
      1 teaspoon black pepper

Heat the oil in a large pot over low heat. Add the garlic, onions, curry powder, cayenne pepper, bay leaf, and parsley and cook uncovered over low heat, stirring frequently, for 10 minutes. Add the water, cover, and bring to a boil. Stir in the lentils and rice. Cook uncovered over low heat, stirring frequently, for 1½ hours, until tender. Stir in the peas, chutney, salt, and pepper. Continue cooking over low heat for 30 minutes, stirring frequently. Taste for seasoning.

Lentils and Tubetini

SERVES 6

This soup is very plain, yet delicious. My mother and my grandmother often made it for me when I was a child. For me, it's comfort food.

    4 quarts water
    1 pound lentils, picked over
    1 cup (packed) chopped flat-leaf parsley
    ¼ cup plus 2 tablespoons olive oil
    1 bunch celery with tops, chopped
    ¼ cup chopped fresh basil leaves or ½ teaspoon dried basil
    8 large cloves garlic, minced
    ⅓ pound cooked tubetini (little pasta tubes)
    ½ teaspoon black pepper
       Salt to taste

Bring the water to a boil over high heat in a large covered pot. Add the lentils, parsley, olive oil, celery, basil, and garlic. Cook uncovered over medium heat, stirring frequently, for 45 minutes. Lower the heat and simmer an additional 45 minutes, stirring frequently. Stir in the cooked pasta, pepper, and salt. Continue cooking for 5 minutes. Taste for seasoning.

Mushroom Barley Soup with Lima Beans

SERVES 6

This soup was inspired by one of our many terrific employees at **Claire's**. Sally remembers her grandmother making a "meaty" mushroom and barley soup she loved. Here is my meatless interpretation. Sally says it's as good as her grandmother's.

    4 quarts water
    ½ pound lima beans, picked over
    ½ pound barley
    6 carrots, chopped
    ½ bunch celery, chopped
    ¼ cup chopped flat-leaf parsley
    1 small onion, chopped
    3 cloves garlic, chopped
    6 tablespoons (¾ stick) butter
    ½ teaspoon dried basil
    ¼ teaspoon nutmeg
    1 bay leaf
    3 potatoes, diced
    1 pound mushrooms, sliced
      Salt to taste
    1 teaspoon black pepper

In a large covered pot, bring the water to a boil. Stir in the lima beans and cook over medium heat uncovered for 30 minutes. Add the barley, carrots, celery, parsley, onion, garlic, butter, basil, nutmeg, and bay leaf. Cook uncovered over medium heat, stirring frequently, for 1½ to 2 hours, until the lima beans are tender. Stir in the potatoes, mushrooms, salt, and pepper. Continue cooking over low heat, stirring frequently, for 30 minutes, or until the soup is thick. Taste for seasoning.

Pasta e Fagioli

SERVES 6

Pasta e fagioli (pasta fa'sool) was what we ate for dinner at home every Friday during Lent. When we started making it at **Claire's** in 1975, most of our non-Italian customers had never eaten it before. They loved it so much that we now make it at least once a week.

　　3 quarts water
　　1 pound great northern beans, picked over
　　1 cup chopped flat-leaf parsley
　　6 cloves garlic, chopped
　　4 or 5 basil leaves, chopped, or 1 teaspoon dried basil
　　2 teaspoons fennel seeds
　　1 teaspoon crushed red pepper flakes
　　1 bay leaf
　　⅓ cup olive oil
One 28-ounce can whole tomatoes in juice, crushed with your hands
　　　　Salt to taste
　　1 teaspoon black pepper
　　½ pound cooked little pasta (try ditalini, tubetini, or little shells)

Put the water, beans, parsley, garlic, basil, fennel seeds, red pepper flakes, and bay leaf in a large covered pot. Bring to a boil. Lower the heat to medium and cook uncovered for 1 hour, stirring every 10 minutes or so. Add the olive oil and tomatoes. Continue cooking, stirring frequently, for another 1½ hours, until the beans are soft and the broth is thick. Add the salt and pepper. Stir in the pasta and continue cooking for 1 minute. Taste for seasoning.

White Beans with Broccoli and Potatoes

SERVES 6

We cook the beans until they are soft and creamy, which gives this soup a rich taste without adding extra fat.

    4 quarts water
    1 pound great northern beans, picked over
    4 tablespoons (½ stick) butter or margarine
    ¼ cup olive oil
    8 cloves garlic, chopped
    ¼ cup chopped flat-leaf parsley
    1 bay leaf
    ½ teaspoon dried basil
    ½ teaspoon crushed red pepper flakes
    ½ teaspoon fennel seeds
    4 large potatoes, diced
    1 bunch broccoli, bottom 1 inch of stems removed and discarded, chopped
      Salt to taste
    1 teaspoon black pepper

Bring the water to a boil in a large covered pot. Add the beans, butter or margarine, olive oil, garlic, parsley, bay leaf, basil, red pepper flakes, and fennel seeds. Cook uncovered over medium heat for 1½ hours, stirring occasionally, until the beans are tender. Stir in the potatoes and the broccoli stems, reserving the florets, and continue cooking over medium heat for 30 minutes, stirring frequently. Stir in the broccoli florets, salt, and pepper. Cook for 10 minutes. Taste for seasoning.

Minestrone 1

SERVES 8

Minestrones are tasty and robust and can be made with any number of different vegetables and beans. We sometimes add green peas, fresh corn, spinach, or kale, or use only chickpeas or navy (pea) beans.

    4 quarts water
    ½ pound red kidney beans, picked over
    ½ pound great northern beans, picked over
    ¼ pound lentils, picked over
    1 small onion, chopped
    6 cloves garlic, chopped
    ¼ cup chopped parsley
    ½ small cabbage, chopped
One 8-ounce can whole tomatoes, crushed with your hands
    1 cup olive oil
    ¼ teaspoon dried oregano
    ¼ teaspoon dried basil
    3 carrots, diced
    ½ bunch celery, diced
    1 zucchini, diced
    1 potato, diced
    1 cup chopped broccoli florets
      Salt to taste
    1 teaspoon black pepper
    ½ cup cooked tubetini (little pasta tubes)

Bring the water to a boil in a large pot. Add the kidney beans and cook uncovered over medium heat for 30 minutes. Add the great northern beans and continue cooking, stirring occasionally, for 1 hour. Add the lentils, onion, garlic, parsley, cabbage, tomatoes, olive oil, oregano, basil, carrots, and celery and continue cooking, uncovered, for 1 hour. When the kidney beans are soft, add the zucchini, potato, broccoli, salt, and pepper and continue cooking over low heat for 30 minutes. Stir in the pasta and taste for seasoning.

Minestrone II

SERVES 8

My grandmother often added white rice to her minestrone. I don't think she'd heard of brown rice, but I know she would approve because it is more nutritious than white rice and has a great nutty flavor.

    4 quarts water
    ¼ pound kidney beans, picked over
    ½ pound navy (pea) beans, picked over
    8 cloves garlic, chopped
    1 small head cabbage, chopped
    ¼ cup chopped parsley
    ¾ cup olive oil
    2 small onions, chopped
    ½ bunch celery, diced
One 8-ounce can whole tomatoes, crushed with your hands
    ¼ teaspoon dried basil
    ¼ teaspoon dried oregano
    ½ cup brown rice, uncooked
    2 medium potatoes, diced
One 10-ounce box frozen green peas
    ½ cup grated Romano
    1 teaspoon black pepper

Bring the water to a boil in a large covered pot. Add the kidney beans and cook over medium heat for 1 hour. Add the navy beans, garlic, cabbage, parsley, olive oil, onions, celery, tomatoes, basil, oregano, and rice. Simmer uncovered for 1½ hours, until the beans are tender. Add the potatoes and green peas and continue simmering for 15 minutes. Stir in the cheese and pepper. Taste for seasoning.

My Mother-in-Law's Special Holiday Soup

SERVES 8

My mother-in-law prepares this delicious soup for me to replace her usual holiday *minestre*, which includes meat. Our entire family enjoys it.

    4 quarts water
    1 pound navy (pea) beans, picked over
    1 cup olive oil
    8 cloves garlic, chopped
    1 small onion, chopped
    1 small green cabbage, chopped
    ¼ cup chopped parsley
    4 carrots, diced
    ⅓ bunch celery, diced
One 8-ounce can whole tomatoes, crushed with your hands
    ¼ teaspoon dried basil
    1 small zucchini, diced
    2 cups finely chopped cauliflower
    ½ cup finely chopped broccoli
    1 potato, diced
    ½ head escarole, chopped
    1 cup chopped spinach
      Salt to taste
    1 teaspoon black pepper
    ½ cup cooked small pasta (tubetini or ditalini)

Bring the water to a boil in a large pot. Add the navy beans and cook uncovered over medium heat for 45 minutes. Add the olive oil, garlic, onion, cabbage, parsley, carrots, celery, tomatoes, and basil. Simmer uncovered, stirring frequently, until the beans are nearly tender, about 1½ hours. Add the zucchini, cauliflower, broccoli, potato, escarole, spinach, salt, and pepper. Continue simmering, stirring frequently, for 30 minutes. Stir in the pasta. Taste for seasoning.

Tomato Barley Soup

SERVES 6

This ever-popular soup is quick, easy to prepare, and delicious.

    2 quarts water
Two 28-ounce cans whole tomatoes, crushed with your hands
    ¼ cup chopped parsley
    2 large onions, chopped
    5 cloves garlic, chopped
    ¼ cup olive oil
    ¼ teaspoon dried dill weed
    ¼ teaspoon dried basil
    ½ pound barley
      Salt to taste
    1 teaspoon black pepper

Bring the water to a boil in a large covered pot. Add the remaining ingredients and cook uncovered over medium heat, stirring frequently, for 1¼ hours, or until the barley is soft and the soup is thick. Taste for seasoning.

Tomato-Potato-Pea and Pasta Soup

SERVES 6

This soup is so flavorful and thick, it could double as an Italian stew. Serve it with chunks of hard-crusted bread for dunking.

>   3 quarts water
> Two 28-ounce cans whole tomatoes, crushed with your hands
>   2 large onions, sliced
>   ¼ cup chopped parsley
>   6 cloves garlic, chopped
>   ¾ cup olive oil
>   ¼ teaspoon dried basil
>   6 large potatoes, diced
> One 10-ounce box frozen peas
>   ¼ pound cooked medium pasta shells
>   Salt to taste
>   1 teaspoon black pepper

Bring the water to a boil in a large covered soup pot. Add the tomatoes, onions, parsley, garlic, olive oil, and basil. Cook uncovered over medium heat, stirring frequently, for 1 hour. Add the potatoes and continue cooking for 45 minutes, stirring frequently. Add the peas and cook for 15 minutes. Stir in the pasta, salt, and pepper. Taste for seasoning.

Cream of Onion Soup

SERVES 6

Our customers love this soup. We make it infrequently, because it contains butter, milk, cheese, *and* cream.

8 tablespoons (1 stick) butter, cut into pieces
8 large onions, chopped
¼ cup chopped parsley
½ cup flour
1 quart warm water
1 quart milk
2 cups heavy cream
½ cup grated Romano
1 cup grated Swiss cheese
¼ teaspoon nutmeg
1 teaspoon black pepper

In a large pot with a lid, melt the butter over low heat. Add the onions and parsley. Cover and cook over low heat, stirring frequently, until the onions are very soft, about 30 minutes. Stir in the flour, combining well. Simmer uncovered over low heat, stirring frequently, for 10 minutes. Stir in the water and cook, stirring frequently, for 30 minutes. Stir in the milk, cream, cheeses, nutmeg, and pepper. Mix well and heat thoroughly, stirring frequently, until slightly thickened. Taste for seasoning.

My Mom's Onion Soup

SERVES 6

This is what Mom makes for us at the first sign of a cold, and she always knows best. Besides, this medicine is not at all hard to swallow.

½ cup olive oil
10 large onions, chopped
¼ cup chopped parsley
3 quarts water
Salt to taste
1 teaspoon black pepper

Heat the olive oil in an uncovered large pot over low heat. Add the onions and parsley. Cover and cook over low heat, stirring frequently, for 30 minutes, until the onions are golden brown. Add the water and raise the heat to medium. Cook covered, stirring frequently, for 30 minutes. Add the salt and pepper. Taste for seasoning.

Potato-Corn Chowder

SERVES 4

We love chowders at **Claire's.** This one is terrific, but it's higher in cholesterol than our bean soups, so we don't serve it very often. But when we do our customers happily indulge.

    8 tablespoons (1 stick) butter, cut into pieces
    1 large onion, chopped
    6 cloves garlic, chopped
    ¼ cup chopped parsley
      Corn kernels cut from 6 ears, or 2 cups frozen kernels
    6 large potatoes, diced
    1 quart water
    ¼ teaspoon dried dill weed
    1 quart milk
    1 cup heavy cream
    ½ teaspoon dried thyme
      Salt to taste
    1 teaspoon black pepper

Melt the butter over low heat in an uncovered large pot. Add the onion, garlic, parsley, corn, and potatoes. Cover and cook over very low heat for 30 minutes, stirring frequently. Add the water and bring to a boil. Simmer uncovered for 30 to 45 minutes, until the potatoes are tender. Stir in the dill weed, milk, cream, thyme, salt, and pepper. Simmer, stirring frequently, for 15 minutes. Taste for seasoning.

French Peasant Soup

SERVES 8

This is a hearty and savory stew-like soup.

    4 quarts water
   12 ounces great northern beans, picked over
    1 small onion, chopped
    8 cloves garlic, minced
   ½ cup olive oil
   ¼ teaspoon dried thyme
    1 bay leaf
   ¼ teaspoon dried basil
    6 carrots, chopped
   ½ bunch celery, chopped
   ¼ cup chopped parsley
    4 tablespoons (½ stick) butter
    1 small head green cabbage, chopped
    5 medium potatoes, diced
      Salt to taste
    1 teaspoon black pepper

Bring the water to a boil in a large covered pot. Add the beans, reduce the heat to medium, and cook uncovered for 30 minutes, stirring frequently. Add the onion, garlic, olive oil, thyme, bay leaf, basil, carrots, celery, parsley, butter, and cabbage. Bring to a boil, then reduce the heat to low and simmer for 1½ hours, stirring frequently, until the beans are nearly tender. Add the potatoes, salt, and pepper. Continue simmering for 30 to 45 minutes, until the beans are very soft and the soup is thick. Taste for seasoning.

French Vegetable Bisque

SERVES 6

This is our vegetarian version of a rich lobster bisque, and it is a favorite among the staff. Everyone loves its flavor—creamy and spicy.

      8 tablespoons (1 stick) butter, cut into pieces
      1 large onion, chopped
      4 shallots, chopped
      ¼ cup chopped parsley
      ½ teaspoon dried thyme
      4 carrots, chopped
      ½ bunch celery, chopped
      1 large potato, diced
      1 cup white wine
Two 28-ounce cans whole tomatoes, crushed with your hands
      1 zucchini, chopped
      1 cup brown rice, uncooked
      ½ bunch broccoli, bottom 1 inch removed and discarded, chopped
      1 quart milk
      1 cup heavy cream
      2 or 3 shakes Tabasco
      Salt to taste
      1 teaspoon black pepper

Melt the butter in a large uncovered pot. Add the onion, shallots, parsley, and thyme. Cover and cook over low heat, stirring frequently, for 15 minutes, or until the onions are tender. Add the carrots, celery, potato, wine, tomatoes, and zucchini. Bring to a boil over medium heat, uncovered. Lower the heat, stir in the rice, and simmer, stirring frequently, about 1 hour, until the rice is cooked. Stir in the broccoli and continue cooking for 15 minutes. Stir in the milk, cream, Tabasco, salt, and pepper. Heat through. Taste for seasoning.

Curried Cream of Cauliflower Soup

SERVES 6

Curry and cauliflower were meant to be together, as far as I'm concerned. This soup will make you agree.

8 tablespoons (1 stick) butter, cut into pieces
1 large onion, chopped
2 large heads cauliflower, chopped
2 large potatoes, peeled and chopped
1 tablespoon curry powder
Pinch cayenne pepper
1 bay leaf
1 quart milk
1 cup heavy cream
Salt to taste
1 teaspoon black pepper
½ cup bottled mango chutney (found in the condiment section of most supermarkets)

Melt the butter in a large uncovered pot over low heat. Add the onion, cauliflower, and potatoes. Sprinkle with the curry powder and cayenne pepper and stir to combine. Cover and cook over very low heat for 30 minutes, stirring frequently. Add the bay leaf and water to cover, plus 3 inches. Stir to mix well. Raise the heat to medium, cover, and bring to a boil, then lower the heat and simmer for 1 hour, until the cauliflower is soft. Use a long-handled potato masher to mash the soup in the pot. Stir in the milk, cream, salt, pepper, and chutney. Heat through. Taste for seasoning.

White Bean Soup with Sweet Potato

SERVES 6

We look forward to serving this soup every fall and enjoy it throughout the winter at **Claire's**.

    4 quarts water
    1 pound great northern beans, picked over
    2 bay leaves
    ¾ cup olive oil
    10 cloves garlic, chopped
    1 cup chopped parsley
    6 medium sweet potatoes, peeled and diced
    ¼ teaspoon dried basil or 10 leaves fresh basil, chopped
        Salt to taste
    1 teaspoon black pepper

Bring the water to a boil in a large covered pot. Add the beans and bay leaves. Cook uncovered over medium heat for 1½ to 2 hours, stirring occasionally, until the beans are soft.

Meanwhile, in a large skillet, heat the olive oil over low heat. Add the garlic and cook, stirring frequently, for 5 minutes. Add the parsley, sweet potatoes, and basil. Sprinkle with salt and pepper. Cook uncovered over low heat for 20 minutes, stirring frequently, until the sweet potatoes are tender. Spoon the sweet potato mixture into the cooking beans. Continue cooking for 30 minutes, stirring frequently. Taste for seasoning.

Kidney Bean Soup with Butternut Squash

SERVES 6

I based this soup on my memory of a delicious dish my Aunt Rose made as a sauce for linguine. She was and still is one of the best cooks in our family. This is a perfect soup for a cold winter night.

    4 quarts water
    1 pound kidney beans, picked over
    2 bay leaves
    ¾ cup olive oil
  10 cloves garlic, chopped
    2 butternut squash, cut in half lengthwise, seeded, peeled, and cubed
    1 bunch flat-leaf parsley, chopped
    ½ teaspoon dried basil or 10 leaves fresh basil, chopped
       Salt to taste
    1 teaspoon black pepper

Bring the water to a boil in a large covered pot. Add the beans and bay leaves. Cook over medium heat, uncovered, for 1½ hours, stirring frequently, until the beans are nearly tender.

In a large skillet, heat the olive oil over low heat. Add the garlic and cook, stirring frequently, for 5 minutes, until it softens and is barely golden. Add the squash, parsley, basil, salt, and pepper. Cook uncovered over low heat about 20 minutes, stirring frequently, until slightly softened. Spoon the squash mixture into the pot of beans, scraping up the bits that cling to the bottom of the skillet. Simmer for 45 minutes, stirring frequently, until the squash and beans are soft and the soup is thick. Taste for seasoning.

Spring and Summer Vegetable Soup

SERVES 6

We take advantage of the new crop of asparagus and corn each spring to make this lovely light soup.

    8 tablespoons (1 stick) butter
    2 shallots, chopped
    3 leeks, thoroughly washed and chopped
    1 bunch asparagus, bottom 1 inch removed and discarded, tips separated, stems cut into ½-inch lengths
    1 medium onion, chopped
    6 carrots, chopped
    ½ bunch celery, chopped
    4 potatoes, diced
    1 cup chopped parsley
    4 quarts water
    1 teaspoon dried tarragon
    1 bay leaf
    ¼ cup brown rice, uncooked
    4 small summer squash, diced
    Corn kernels cut from 3 ears, or one 10-ounce box frozen kernels
One 10-ounce bag fresh spinach, chopped
    Salt to taste
    1 teaspoon black pepper

Melt the butter in a large pot over low heat. Add the shallots and leeks and cook over low heat for 15 minutes, stirring frequently. Add the chopped stems of the asparagus, the onions, carrots, celery, potatoes, and parsley. Cook over low heat, stirring frequently, for 15 minutes. Add the water, tarragon, and bay leaf and bring to a boil. Add the rice, lower the heat, cover, and simmer for 1 hour, stirring frequently. Add the squash, corn, spinach, salt, pepper, and asparagus tips. Continue simmering uncovered for 15 minutes. Taste for seasoning.

Fall and Winter Vegetable Soup

SERVES 6

This is a savory soup to enjoy on a cold winter night.

        8 tablespoons (1 stick) butter, cut into pieces
        1 large onion, chopped
        3 large cloves garlic, chopped
        6 medium carrots, chopped
        4 medium parsnips, chopped
        ½ bunch celery, chopped
        2 white potatoes, diced
        2 sweet potatoes, peeled and diced
        1 medium cauliflower, cored and chopped
        1 cup chopped parsley
        4 quarts water
          Salt to taste
        1 teaspoon black pepper
        ½ teaspoon dried sage
        ½ teaspoon dried thyme
        ½ teaspoon fennel seeds
        1 bay leaf
  One 10-ounce box frozen green peas

Melt the butter in a large pot over low heat. Add the onion, garlic, carrots, parsnips, celery, white and sweet potatoes, cauliflower, and parsley. Cover and cook over low heat for 20 minutes, stirring frequently. Add the water, salt, pepper, sage, thyme, fennel seeds, and bay leaf. Cover and bring to a boil, then reduce heat to medium. Simmer uncovered for 1¼ hours, stirring frequently. Add the peas. Cook 15 minutes, stirring frequently. Taste for seasoning.

New England Vegetable Chowder

SERVES 6

We replaced the fish and seafood with chunks of vegetables for this delicious interpretation of a traditional favorite.

8 tablespoons (1 stick) butter, cut into pieces
1 large onion, chopped
4 medium carrots
½ bunch celery, chopped
4 medium potatoes, diced
   Corn kernels cut from 3 ears, or one 10-ounce box frozen kernels
1 teaspoon dried thyme
2 quarts water
   Salt to taste
1 teaspoon black pepper
1 bay leaf
1 cup heavy cream
1 quart milk

Melt the butter in a large pot over low heat. Add the onion, carrots, celery, potatoes, corn, and thyme. Cover and cook or 20 minutes, stirring frequently. Add the water, salt, pepper, and bay leaf. Raise the heat to medium, cover, and bring to a boil, stirring frequently. Cook over low heat for 1 hour, stirring frequently. Stir in the cream and milk. Cook for 10 minutes. Taste for seasoning.

Appetizers and Sandwiches

The dishes in this chapter can stand alone for a terrific lunch, be divided into tasty appetizers, or be combined with the soups in the preceding chapter for great wholesome dinners.

We've never bothered with a large selection of appetizers at **Claire's.** Our portions are substantial, and our dinners are served with a mug of hearty soup or a small salad and a little loaf of our honey-wheat and country white bread. People don't generally pass up our famous soups, and who can resist homemade bread? We sometimes offer large portions of these appetizers as entrees. I've served them at many parties, and everyone has always enjoyed them.

My mom never cared for "lunch meats." She made us sandwiches of cooked vegetables for lunch, usually teamed with soup. Most of the sandwiches in this book are from my memory of lunches she and my grandmother prepared for us. These, along with ideas we get from our staff and customers, are the sandwiches we serve at **Claire's.** We make our sandwiches on wheat pita, bagels, or thick slices of our homemade honey-wheat or challah breads. While most of our sandwich fillings are best as is, we sometimes add a special mustard, mayonnaise, or puree. Interesting mustards can be readily found in the condiment section of most supermarkets and gourmet shops; or you can make spreads for your sandwiches, starting with store-bought mustard or mayonnaise and adding spices, lemon juice, herbs, and so on. It's always a good idea to have extra sandwich fillings on hand for unexpected guests and unexpected appetites, and it's easy to do. Start out with a good mustard and mix in dill or chopped capers or finely minced sun-dried tomatoes, honey, or horseradish. Maybe add a little mayonnaise. Experiment creatively and you can enjoy countless delicious choices.

Stuffed Mushroom Caps 1

SERVES 8

These are cholesterol-free, lactose-free little gems. They smell so good when they come out of the oven that you will have to taste-test one as soon as it is cool enough to pop into your mouth.

16 medium mushrooms, stems removed and reserved for another use
½ of a small loaf French bread, cut into pieces
3 ribs celery, diced
10 oil-cured black olives, pitted and chopped
3 tablespoons olive oil
   Pinch oregano
4 cloves garlic, minced
2 tablespoons minced parsley
   Salt to taste
¼ teaspoon black pepper

Preheat the oven to 375 degrees. Rinse and dry the mushroom caps while you prepare the stuffing. Place the bread in a bowl and run hot water over it to cover. Drain in a colander and carefully squeeze out as much water as possible. Turn into a bowl and set aside.

Boil the celery in water to cover, stirring frequently, until it is crisp-tender and most of the water is absorbed, 3 to 7 minutes. Drain and add the celery to the drained bread. Add the remaining ingredients and mix well. Taste for seasoning.

Mound the stuffing in the mushroom caps. Place in a single layer in a baking pan. Pour in ¼ cup water. Cover with foil and bake for 45 minutes. Remove the foil, add water if needed, and continue baking, uncovered, for 15 minutes, until the mushrooms are tender. Serve hot.

Stuffed Mushroom Caps II

SERVES 4

Use bite-sized mushrooms for appetizers or huge mushrooms if you're serving them for lunch or dinner. Team them up with black bean salad served warm, a tossed vegetable salad, and some good wheat bread for a perfect weeknight dinner. The mushrooms can be prepared a day in advance. Cover and refrigerate, then bake as directed.

> 12 medium mushrooms, stems removed and reserved for another use
> ½ of a 10-ounce bag fresh spinach, rinsed, drained, and chopped fine (about 3 packed cups)
> 2 tablespoons Dijon mustard
> 2 tablespoons nonfat mayonnaise
> 4 ounces shredded low-fat cheddar
> ¼ cup chopped walnuts
> 2 tablespoons plain bread crumbs
> 1 teaspoon black pepper

Preheat the oven to 400 degrees. Wash and dry the mushroom caps. In a bowl, combine the spinach, mustard, mayonnaise, cheddar, walnuts, bread crumbs, and pepper. Taste for seasoning. Mound the stuffing in the mushroom caps.

Arrange in a single layer in a baking pan. Pour in water to ¼ inch deep. Cover with a foil tent so that the foil does not touch the mushroom stuffing. Bake, covered, for 30 minutes, then uncover and continue cooking for 10 minutes, or until the mushrooms are tender.

Mrs. Sav's Hot Antipasto

SERVES 8 TO 10

Chrissy "Sav," whom we have had the pleasure and good fortune to employ since her high school days, is now our general manager at **Claire's.** Many years ago she brought in her mother's recipe for antipasto. We have changed it many times over the years and have enjoyed it each new way. This is our latest version. It makes a lovely appetizer, lunch, or dinner.

½ bunch celery, sliced into ¼-inch pieces
1 bunch broccoli, chopped (discard bottom 1 inch of stems)
1 small zucchini, sliced into 1-inch pieces
1 small red onion, sliced into ¼-inch rings
1 small yellow squash, sliced into 1-inch pieces
3 cloves garlic, minced
1 red bell pepper, seeded and sliced into ½-inch ribs
1 box frozen sliced artichoke hearts
8 medium mushrooms, sliced
¼ cup sliced black olives
3 tablespoons olive oil
¼ cup plain bread crumbs
¼ cup grated Romano
¼ cup chopped parsley
  Salt to taste
¼ teaspoon black pepper

Preheat the oven to 350 degrees. Place all the ingredients in a bowl and combine well. Turn into a rectangular glass baking dish, cover with foil, and bake for 45 minutes, then uncover and continue baking for 15 minutes. Serve hot.

Tofu Sausage Kebobs with Honey Mustard

SERVES 8 TO 10

Tofu sausage creates quite a stir. It looks and tastes like traditional sausage, but contains no meat or cholesterol. You can find it in most health-food stores.

> 1 pound tofu sausage links
> 1 small pineapple, trimmed and cut into cubes
> ¼ cup packed brown sugar
> 1 cup honey mustard

Preheat the oven to 400 degrees. Heat a nonstick skillet sprayed with non-stick cooking spray over medium-high heat and cook the tofu sausage links until they are golden brown and slightly firm to the touch. Turn onto a cutting board. While they cool enough to cut into quarters, toss the pineapple in the brown sugar to coat.

Using either metal skewers or wooden skewers that have been soaked in cold water for 30 minutes to prevent burning, thread ¼ of a sausage link with a pineapple cube on each skewer, then lay the skewers in a single layer on a cookie sheet. Bake for 15 minutes, until hot. Serve with the honey mustard for dipping.

Hummus

SERVES 8 TO 10

We love hummus at **Claire's**. It's great for dipping or in a sandwich. This version has cayenne pepper and Tabasco to give it a little more zip than our hummus sandwich filling. Either way, it's cholesterol-free and delicious.

    1 pound chickpeas
    1 cup tahini (sesame paste, found in health-food stores)
    ¼ cup olive oil
       Juice of 2 lemons
    3 tablespoons water
       Large pinch cayenne pepper
       Dash Tabasco
    4 cloves garlic, chopped
       Salt to taste
    ½ cup chopped parsley
    ¼ teaspoon paprika

Soak the chickpeas in a large pot overnight in 10 cups of water. Add fresh water to cover by 2 inches, then boil for 2 hours or until soft, adding water as necessary. Drain.

Place all the ingredients except the parsley and paprika in the bowl of a food processor. Puree until smooth. Taste for seasoning. Turn into a bowl and sprinkle with the parsley and paprika. Serve with pita triangles for dipping.

A.M.M. (Avocado, Mozzarella, and Mushroom) Sandwich

MAKES 4 SANDWICHES

Pita bread sandwiches are very popular, and this is our number one seller at **Claire's.** It is definitely a sandwich to eat with a fork.

    4 whole-wheat pita breads
    1 small head romaine, rinsed and torn into pieces
    1 carrot, shredded
    1 tomato, cut into 8 wedges
    1 small onion, sliced
    12 small mushrooms, sliced
    1 ripe avocado, peeled and sliced
    8 ounces shredded low-fat mozzarella
       Tahini Dressing (see page 121), or your favorite dressing
       Alfalfa sprouts

Preheat the oven to 350 degrees. Cut ½ inch off the edge of each pita. Open wide. Wrap each pita in foil, leaving the top open. Stuff each pita with layers of romaine, carrot, tomato, onion, mushrooms, avocado, and mozzarella, ending with the mozzarella on top. Arrange in a single layer in a baking pan. Bake for 5 minutes, until the cheese is melted but not brown. Set each sandwich in a bowl. Top with dressing and alfalfa sprouts and serve immediately.

Vegetarian Reuben

MAKES 4 SANDWICHES

This substantial open-faced sandwich is so tasty that you will never miss the corned beef.

4 large slices of good rye bread
4 tablespoons Dijon mustard
2 large ripe tomatoes, sliced into 8 rounds
1 cup sauerkraut, drained
4 tablespoons Russian dressing, homemade or store-bought
4 thin slices Swiss cheese, cut in half

Preheat the oven to 350 degrees. Toast the rye bread. Spread one side of each slice with mustard. Place the slices mustard side up in a single layer on a cookie sheet. Layer each slice of rye with the following, in order: 1 half-slice tomato, 1 slice Swiss cheese, ¼ cup sauerkraut, and 1 tablespoon Russian dressing.

Bake for 20 minutes, until the sauerkraut is hot. Top each sandwich with a slice of tomato and a half-slice of cheese. Continue baking for 5 to 10 minutes, until the cheese is melted.

Eggplant and Tomato Sandwich Filling

MAKES 6 SANDWICHES

You can prepare this delicious sandwich filling up to three days in advance and have leftovers on hand for snacks or unexpected guests. We serve it open-faced with melted mozzarella on top, but it also tastes great with fontina or provolone.

¼ cup olive oil
1 large eggplant, diced
4 cloves garlic, minced
3 green bell peppers, seeded and chopped
1 large tomato, chopped
¼ cup water
½ 10-ounce bag fresh spinach, chopped
1 tablespoon red-wine vinegar
1 teaspoon capers, rinsed and chopped
½ cup chopped fresh basil
Salt and black pepper to taste

In a large skillet, heat the oil over low heat. Add the eggplant and garlic and cook, stirring frequently for 5 minutes. Add the peppers and tomato. Continue cooking for 5 minutes, stirring frequently. Add the water, raise the heat to medium, and cover. Bring to a low boil and cook for 20 minutes, stirring frequently, until the eggplant is tender. Stir in the spinach, vinegar, capers, basil, salt, and pepper. Cook uncovered for 10 minutes, stirring frequently, until the liquid evaporates and the mixture is stew-like.

To serve, spoon over French bread or the bread of your choice. If you wish, top with shredded mozzarella and broil or bake at 375 degrees until the cheese melts.

Artichoke Hearts, Cucumber, and Tomato on Black Bread with Sun-Dried Tomato Puree

MAKES 4 SANDWICHES

This combination was inspired by Karis, one of our many great managers, who loves artichoke hearts. They make a delicious sandwich when combined with thinly sliced cucumbers and ripe tomatoes, and the sun-dried tomato puree adds just the right zip.

> 10 sun-dried tomatoes, packed in oil (found in the gourmet section of most supermarkets)
> 2 tablespoons olive oil
> One 10-ounce box frozen artichoke hearts, defrosted and thinly sliced
> ½ English (seedless) cucumber, thinly sliced
> 1 medium tomato, thinly sliced
> Salt and black pepper to taste
> 8 slices Russian black bread or pumpernickel

Place the sun-dried tomatoes with the oil clinging to them plus the 2 tablespoons olive oil in a blender. Puree until smooth. Spread the puree on one side of each slice of bread. Layer the artichoke hearts, cucumber, and tomato slices on 4 slices of the bread. Sprinkle with salt and pepper. Top with the remaining 4 slices of bread.

Broccoli-Mushroom Melt

MAKES 4 SANDWICHES

Vanessa has worked at **Claire's** since her first year at college. She and her mother are also two of our best customers. This is Vanessa's (and a lot of other people's) favorite sandwich.

    ¼ cup olive oil
    4 large cloves garlic, minced
    1 large bunch broccoli, bottom 1 inch of stems removed and discarded
    ¼ teaspoon crushed red pepper flakes
    ½ pound mushrooms, sliced
       Salt to taste
    ¼ teaspoon black pepper
    1 long loaf French bread, cut into 4 pieces, then split lengthwise
    4 ounces Monterey Jack cheese, shredded

Preheat the oven to 400 degrees. Cut the broccoli stems into ¼-inch slices and chop the florets into small pieces.

In a large skillet, heat the oil over low heat. Add the garlic and cook for 2 minutes, stirring frequently; do not let it brown. Add the broccoli stems and red pepper flakes. Raise the heat to medium and continue cooking for 10 minutes, stirring frequently. Add the mushrooms, broccoli florets, salt, and pepper. Continue cooking for 3 to 5 minutes, stirring frequently, until crisp-tender.

Arrange the bread pieces in a single layer on a cookie sheet. Spoon the broccoli mixture evenly over the bread and top with the cheese. Bake until the cheese is melted.

Hummus and Tomato on Wheat Bread

MAKES 4 SANDWICHES

Hummus is a delicious dip to be served with pita triangles or spread on crackers, and it makes a terrific sandwich filling. Leave a batch in your refrigerator for snacks.

    1 pound chickpeas
    1 cup tahini (sesame paste, found in health-food stores)
    1 cup chopped parsley
    4 cloves garlic, chopped
    4 tablespoons olive oil
      Juice of 2 lemons
      Salt to taste
    ¼ teaspoon black pepper
    1 tablespoon water
    8 slices wheat bread
    1 large tomato, sliced

Soak the chickpeas in a large pot overnight in 10 cups of water. Add fresh water to cover by 2 inches, bring to a boil, reduce heat slightly, and simmer for 2 hours or until soft, adding water as necessary. Drain.

Put all the ingredients except the bread and tomatoes in the bowl of a food processor and process until smooth. Taste for seasoning. Spread on 4 slices of the bread and top with the tomato slices and the remaining slices of bread.

Tomato, Onion, and Basil on French Bread

MAKES 4 SANDWICHES

This is a popular summer sandwich at **Claire's.** Our customers know we have only ten weeks to enjoy enough native tomatoes to carry us through until next season, so they are eager to get their fill of these magnificent vine-ripened beauties.

    3 large ripe tomatoes, sliced into ¼-inch pieces
    1 small yellow onion, sliced into very thin rings
    12 leaves fresh basil
    3 tablespoons olive oil
    1 tablespoon balsamic vinegar
       Salt and black pepper to taste
    1 loaf French bread, cut into 4 pieces and then split lengthwise

Place the tomatoes, onion, and basil in a bowl. Sprinkle with the olive oil, balsamic vinegar, salt, and pepper. Toss gently. Taste for seasoning.

Spoon the mixture evenly over 4 of the pieces of bread and top with the remaining 4 pieces. The sandwiches keep well (the flavor actually improves) wrapped and refrigerated for up to 8 hours.

Curried Tofu Salad in Pita

MAKES 4 SANDWICHES

If you like curry, you will love this cholesterol-free sandwich filling. Serve it with mango chutney (found in the condiment section of most supermarkets).

1 pound firm tofu, cut into ½-inch cubes
1 medium carrot, minced
1 rib celery, minced
½ small yellow onion, minced
½ cup cholesterol-free mayonnaise
1 teaspoon curry powder
   Salt to taste
¼ teaspoon black pepper
   Pinch cayenne pepper
2 tablespoons golden raisins
4 whole-wheat pita breads

Place all the ingredients except the pita in a bowl. Mix to combine well. Taste for seasoning.

Cut off the top 1 inch of each pita bread. Open the pita pockets and fill each with ¼ of the tofu mixture.

Roasted Red Peppers with Provolone on Italian Bread

MAKES 4 SANDWICHES

This is a great sandwich. It keeps well for lunch or a picnic. The juices from the peppers are absorbed by the sturdy bread, adding to the flavors. Home-roasted peppers are the best, but a good-quality store-bought variety is a satisfactory substitute when you are pressed for time.

6 bell peppers, red, yellow, green, or a combination
2 tablespoons olive oil
1 tablespoon balsamic vinegar
   Salt and black pepper to taste
4 ounces sliced provolone
1 loaf white Italian bread, cut into 4 pieces and then split lengthwise

Using long metal tongs, hold each pepper over an open flame to roast, charring all sides. Place the peppers in a paper bag or covered bowl and allow to steam for 10 to 15 minutes. When they are cool enough to handle, remove the stems and seeds. Scrape off the charred skin and slice each pepper into 1-inch ribs. Place in a bowl with any juices. Sprinkle with the olive oil, vinegar, salt, and pepper. Taste for seasoning.

Assemble each sandwich using ¼ of the peppers and a slice of provolone. Spoon some of the juices from the peppers over the top.

Stewed Red, Yellow, and Green Peppers on Italian Bread

MAKES 6 SANDWICHES

Peppers stewed with tomatoes, garlic, and onions make a superlative sandwich filling. They keep well for three days. You can enjoy any leftovers tossed with cooked ziti or brown rice for dinner. Peppers also make an especially good topping for veggie burgers. I suggest you make a double batch on weekends to eat all week long.

¼ cup olive oil
4 cloves garlic, minced
1 small red onion, sliced into thin rings
9 bell peppers, red, yellow, and green, seeded and sliced into 1-inch ribs
2 large tomatoes, each cut into 8 wedges
¼ teaspoon dried oregano
Salt and black pepper to taste
3 tablespoons water
1½ loaves Italian bread, cut into 6 pieces and then split lengthwise

In a skillet, heat the olive oil over low heat. Add the garlic, onion, peppers, tomatoes, and oregano. Sprinkle with salt and pepper. Stir to mix. Cover and cook for 10 minutes, stirring frequently. Add the water, raise the heat to medium, and cover. Cook for 15 to 20 minutes, stirring frequently, until the peppers are soft. Taste for seasoning.

Spoon the peppers onto 6 pieces of the bread and top with the remaining 6 pieces. Serve hot or at room temperature.

Zucchini and Eggs in Pita

MAKES 4 SANDWICHES

Here is another great sandwich filling. It is delicious served hot or cold, in a pita or on any good bread. If you wish, you can use cholesterol-free egg substitute.

  3 tablespoons olive oil
  1 small yellow onion, sliced into thin rings
  3 small zucchini, diced
  2 tablespoons water
    Salt to taste
  ½ teaspoon black pepper
  ¼ teaspoon dried oregano
  8 eggs, beaten
  4 whole-wheat or white pita breads

Heat the oil in a nonstick skillet over low heat. Add the onion, cover, and cook for 5 minutes, stirring frequently. Add the zucchini, water, salt, pepper, and oregano. Raise the heat to medium, cover, and continue cooking for 20 minutes, stirring frequently, until the zucchini is crisp-tender. Stir in the beaten eggs, mixing to combine well. Cook about 10 minutes, stirring frequently, until the eggs are completely cooked. Taste for seasoning.

Cut off 1 inch from the top of the pita breads and fill each pocket with one-quarter of the egg mixture.

Open-Faced Pita Pizza

MAKES 4 SANDWICHES

This is a favorite of the children who come to **Claire's,** although marinara sauce on bread with melted cheese seems to appeal to all ages.

    4 whole-wheat pita breads
    1 cup Marinara Sauce (see page 127) or any good tomato sauce (preferably
        homemade), heated
    4 ounces shredded mozzarella
    2 tablespoons grated Parmesan

Preheat the broiler. Place 4 pita rounds on a nonstick cookie sheet. Spoon ¼ cup sauce evenly over each pita. Sprinkle mozzarella and Parmesan evenly over each. Broil until the cheese melts.

Escarole Sauté

MAKES 4 SANDWICHES

Leafy green escarole is so versatile. It is a delicious addition to many soups; the tender inner leaves make a great salad; and when you sauté the leaves, as in this recipe, you have a wonderful sandwich filling. We serve it on thick slices of whole-wheat bread, sometimes with mozzarella melted on top.

    1 large head escarole, bottom 2 inches cut off and discarded
    3 tablespoons olive oil
    3 large cloves garlic, thinly sliced
    ½ teaspoon crushed red pepper flakes
      Salt and black pepper to taste
    6 oil-cured olives, pitted and chopped

Wash the escarole leaves thoroughly. Tear or cut the leaves in half (into about 5-inch pieces). Drain well. Heat the oil in a large skillet over low heat. Add the garlic and red pepper flakes and cook for 3 minutes, stirring frequently, until the garlic is golden. Add the escarole and sprinkle lightly with salt and pepper. Cover and cook over low heat for 15 minutes, stirring frequently. Add the olives and continue cooking uncovered for 15 minutes, stirring frequently, until the escarole is tender enough for your taste.

Broccoli Rabe with Melted Mozzarella

MAKES 4 SANDWICHES

Broccoli rabe, also known as bitter broccoli, is one of my favorite vegetables. We serve it at **Claire's** either over linguine or as a sandwich filling. It's so delicious you will be tempted to taste-test it many times before it reaches the table.

¼ cup olive oil
4 large cloves garlic, thinly sliced
½ teaspoon crushed red pepper flakes
1 large bunch broccoli rabe, bottom 2 inches cut off and discarded
    Salt and black pepper to taste
3 tablespoons water
1 loaf Italian or French bread, cut into 4 pieces and then split lengthwise
4 ounces shredded mozzarella

Heat the oil in a large skillet over low heat. Add the garlic and red pepper flakes. Cook, stirring frequently, for 3 minutes. Add the broccoli rabe and sprinkle with salt and pepper. Add the water, cover, and raise the heat to medium. Continue cooking about 20 minutes, stirring frequently, until the broccoli rabe is tender. Taste for seasoning.

Using a large spoon, divide the broccoli rabe among 4 of the pieces of bread. Sprinkle each with cheese and top with the remaining pieces of bread to allow the heat from the broccoli rabe to melt the cheese slightly.

Peppers and Eggs

MAKES 4 SANDWICHES

This combination produces a delicious sandwich that travels well. It makes a fine lunch for school or work, and we often pack some for lunch in the park or a day of boating.

    3 tablespoons olive oil
    3 bell peppers, red, yellow, green, or a combination, seeded and sliced into
        1-inch ribs
    1 small onion, chopped
    8 eggs, lightly beaten
      Salt to taste
    ½ teaspoon black pepper
    8 slices whole-wheat or Italian bread

Heat the oil in a large skillet over low heat. Add the peppers and onion. Cover and cook for 15 minutes, stirring frequently, until soft. Stir in the eggs, salt, and pepper. Cover and cook for 5 to 10 minutes, stirring frequently, until the eggs are fully cooked.

Divide the filling among 4 sandwiches.

Tzatziki, Tomato, and Onion on Pita

MAKES 4 SANDWICHES

This Greek cucumber-yogurt salad *(tzatziki)* turns tomatoes and onions into a flavorful sandwich filling. Prepare the sauce two to three days ahead and store it in your refrigerator until needed. Note that you will need a cheesecloth to drain the yogurt.

    16 ounces (2 cups) plain nonfat yogurt
     4 cloves garlic, minced
    ½ small cucumber, peeled, minced, and drained
       Salt to taste
    ½ teaspoon black pepper
     2 large, ripe tomatoes, halved, then cut into ¼-inch slices
     1 small onion, sliced into very thin rings
     2 tablespoons olive oil
       Salt and black pepper to taste
    ¼ teaspoon dried oregano
     4 large pita breads

Line a colander with a double layer of cheesecloth and set the colander in a bowl. Spoon the yogurt into the lined colander. Cover with plastic wrap and refrigerate for 1 or 2 hours, until slightly thickened. Turn into a bowl. Stir in the garlic, cucumber, salt, and pepper. Mix to combine well. In a separate bowl, toss together the tomatoes, onion, olive oil, salt, pepper, and oregano.

Spread some *tzatziki* on one half of each pita. Spread the tomato mixture on the other half. Spoon additional *tzatziki* over the tomato mixture. Fold the pita in half to eat.

"Fryers" (Cubanella Peppers with Parmesan)

MAKES 4 SANDWICHES

My mom refers to Cubanella peppers, the six-inch yellow-green peppers (found in most produce sections of supermarkets), as "fryers," because that's how she cooks them. (At **Claire's** and at home, we remove only the stem and eat the pepper, seeds and all.) Fryers can be prepared two days in advance and stored in the refrigerator. They are wonderful hot or cold in a sandwich or just as is. Warning: they can disappear quickly, leaving only an empty plate behind, especially if anyone in your household makes midnight raids on the refrigerator.

¼ cup olive oil
8 Cubanella peppers, rinsed and patted dry
    Salt and black pepper to taste
2 or more tablespoons grated Parmesan

Heat the oil in a large skillet over medium heat. Add the peppers in a single layer. (Use 2 pans or fry in 2 batches if necessary.) Sprinkle lightly with salt and pepper. Cover and fry each side for 3 to 5 minutes, until they are evenly browned and tender. Drain on a cookie sheet lined with paper towels. Arrange on a platter, overlapping slightly, and sprinkle with the Parmesan.

Zucchini Slices with Parmesan

MAKES 8 SANDWICHES

When I was growing up, I remember often visiting my grandmother late on Saturday mornings during the summer. She usually had a platter of zucchini slices set on the counter for me and the others who visited. Today, zucchini slices can be enjoyed at my mother's and my house on many Saturdays during the summer, when there is an overabundance of zucchini. It has become one of our cherished traditions.

¼ cup olive oil
4 medium zucchini (about 8 inches long), sliced lengthwise ¼-inch thick
1 lemon, cut into wedges
2 or 3 tablespoons grated Parmesan
Salt and black pepper to taste

Heat the oil in a large nonstick skillet over medium heat. (The oil is hot enough when a pinch of flour sizzles in it.) Arrange the zucchini slices in the hot oil in a single layer, not touching. Fry both sides until lightly browned, 1 or 2 minutes per side. Drain on a cookie sheet lined with 2 layers of paper towels.

When all the zucchini slices have been fried, arrange them on a large platter. Squeeze lemon juice over the zucchini, then sprinkle with the Parmesan, salt, and pepper. Serve as is or in a sandwich with your favorite bread.

Sautéed Spinach, Shiitake Mushrooms, and Garlic

MAKES 4 SANDWICHES

You can enjoy this sandwich filling either open-faced with Swiss cheese melted on top or between slices of your favorite bread. I like it on thick-crusted Italian bread.

    3 tablespoons olive oil
    2 cloves garlic, minced
    ¼ pound shiitake mushrooms, thinly sliced
One 10-ounce bag fresh spinach, tough stems removed
    Salt and black pepper to taste
    Bread slices

Heat the oil in a large skillet over low heat. Add the garlic and mushrooms, cover, and cook about 5 minutes, stirring frequently, until the mushrooms are barely tender. Add the spinach and sprinkle lightly with salt and pepper. Cover and continue cooking for 5 to 7 minutes, stirring frequently, until the spinach is tender. Remove from the heat.

Use a slotted spoon to transfer the spinach mixture to bread slices.

Eggplant Parmigiana Sandwich

MAKES 4 SANDWICHES

This standby sells quickly whenever we offer it at **Claire's.** I sometimes eat the fried eggplant cutlets, without marinara sauce and cheese, in a sandwich with just a squeeze of lemon. It's a delicious change and travels well.

1 medium eggplant, peeled and sliced into ¼-inch rounds
1 cup flour for dredging the eggplant
6 eggs, lightly beaten
¼ cup chopped parsley
    Salt to taste
½ teaspoon black pepper
½ cup soybean or vegetable oil for frying
1 loaf Italian or French bread, cut into 4 pieces and then split lengthwise
1 cup heated Marinara Sauce (see page 127) or any good tomato sauce
¼ cup grated Parmesan
4 ounces shredded mozzarella

Preheat the oven to 350 degrees. Stack the eggplant slices on a plate and set aside. Measure the flour into a shallow bowl and set aside. Beat the eggs in a bowl, stir in the parsley, and sprinkle with salt and pepper. Beat together lightly. Heat the oil in a large nonstick skillet over low heat. After 2 minutes, test the oil by sprinkling in a pinch of flour, which will sizzle if the oil is hot. Using a fork, dredge a slice of eggplant in the flour, coating both sides. Shake off the excess, then dip both sides in the egg mixture. Lightly shake off the excess and place in the heated oil. Cook each side until golden brown, 1 or 2 minutes per side. Drain on a plate lined with a double thickness of paper towels.

Spread each piece of bread with a little marinara sauce. Divide the eggplant slices among the bottom slices of bread, topping each with a little marinara sauce, grated Parmesan, and shredded mozzarella. Cover each sandwich with the top slice of bread. Arrange the sandwiches on a cookie sheet and bake for 10 to 15 minutes, until the cheese melts.

Breaded Goat Cheese Over Sautéed Arugula

SERVES 4

If you love goat cheese, this sandwich is for you. If you don't have arugula (a bitter, peppery green), spinach is also tasty. We serve this combination open-faced on French bread.

 2 eggs, lightly beaten
 1 tablespoon minced parsley
  Salt and black pepper to taste
 1 cup plain bread crumbs plus more if needed
 5 or 6 ounces chilled goat cheese, sliced into 8 rounds
 3 tablespoons olive oil
 1 clove garlic, minced
 1 bunch arugula or spinach (4 to 6 ounces), cleaned and tough stems
  removed
 1 tablespoon balsamic vinegar
 8 slices French bread

Preheat the oven to 350 degrees. In a bowl, combine the beaten eggs with the parsley. Sprinkle lightly with salt and pepper and mix with a fork. Set aside. Put the bread crumbs in a shallow bowl and set aside. Dip each goat cheese round into the egg mixture, then into the bread crumbs, coating evenly. Add bread crumbs as needed. Arrange the coated cheese rounds in a single layer on a cookie sheet sprayed with nonstick cooking spray. Bake for 20 minutes.

Meanwhile, heat the oil in a large skillet over medium heat. Add the garlic and arugula or spinach and sprinkle with salt and pepper. Cook for 5 to 10 minutes, stirring frequently, until tender. Spoon the balsamic vinegar evenly over the top and stir to combine.

Using a slotted spoon, divide the arugula mixture among the slices of French bread. Top each with a goat cheese round.

Salads

Salads are so good for us, and they can easily be an exciting part of a menu. A salad can be as simple as tossed lettuce, tomato, and onion with a light vinaigrette—or something more inspired, like crisp greens with thin slices of colorful peppers, radicchio, and endive. Add lightly toasted pine nuts and tender navy (pea) beans, then toss with raspberry vinaigrette. As you visit your local farmers' market or roadside stand, or as you walk the produce aisles of your health-food store or neighborhood supermarket, think about all the bounty each season has to offer. Imagine the many combinations of delicious, colorful, and healthful vegetables you can enjoy in a salad, as your time and budget allow. Delight your family, guests, and yourself with a magnificent salad.

Tabouli

SERVES 6

Tabouli is a healthful salad of bulgur (parched cracked wheat). You can find bulgur in health-food stores and in the gourmet section of most supermarkets. Bulgur is a delicious way to add fiber to your diet.

  1 pound bulgur
  1 bunch parsley, leaves chopped, stems discarded
  1 small red onion, coarsely chopped
  ¼ cup olive oil
    Juice of 2 lemons
  2 teaspoons dried mint
    Salt to taste
  ½ teaspoon black pepper

Place the bulgur in a large bowl. Pour over it enough hot water to cover by ¼ inch. Let stand for 1 hour. Add the remaining ingredients, toss well, and taste for seasoning. Serve over torn romaine leaves with tomato and lemon wedges. Drizzle with additional olive oil, if desired.

Avocado, Tomato, and Onion Salad

SERVES 4

This salad is a favorite during the summer months, when the tomatoes are at their best and picnic time is in its prime.

    3 large tomatoes
    1 large avocado, peeled and sliced
    1 small red onion, sliced into thin rings
    3 tablespoons olive oil
      Juice of ½ lemon
    6 fresh basil leaves, chopped
      Salt to taste
    ½ teaspoon black pepper

Cut each tomato in half lengthwise and cut each half into 6 wedges. Cut the avocado in half lengthwise and remove the pit. With a large spoon, carefully scoop out each avocado half. Cut each half into 4 to 6 slices. Place all the ingredients in a bowl and toss gently. Taste for seasoning.

Julienne Vegetable Salad

SERVES 6

This beautiful salad goes well with most lunch and dinner entrees.

3 medium carrots
1 medium zucchini
1 small yellow squash
1 small red onion
1 small yellow bell pepper
1 small red bell pepper
1 small bunch broccoli, bottom 1 inch of stems removed and discarded
¼ cup extra-virgin olive oil
   Freshly grated zest and juice of 1 lemon
1 tablespoon dried dill weed
   Salt to taste
1 teaspoon black pepper

Cut the carrots, zucchini, and squash into matchsticks 1½ inches long. Place in a large bowl. Slice the onion into ⅛-inch rings, separate, and add to the cut vegetables. Seed and slice the peppers into ¼-inch ribs and add to the cut vegetables. Remove and discard the bottom 1 inch of the broccoli stems. Slice the stems into matchsticks 1½ inches long. Add to the cut vegetables. Chop the broccoli florets into small pieces and add to the cut vegetables. Add the olive oil, lemon zest and juice, dill weed, salt, and pepper. Toss well. Taste for seasoning.

Greek Salad

SERVES 4

You can enjoy this salad year-round. It also makes a tasty filling for a pita pocket.

3 bell peppers, 1 each red, yellow, and green, seeded and sliced
1 small red onion, sliced into thin rings
1 English (seedless) cucumber, peeled and sliced into ¼-inch rounds
1 bunch broccoli, bottom 1 inch of stems removed and discarded, chopped into small pieces
8 to 12 Greek olives, drained
2 tomatoes, cut in half and then sliced
8 ounces feta cheese, chopped

Dressing:

⅓ cup olive oil
2 tablespoons lemon juice
1 tablespoon red-wine vinegar
½ teaspoon dried oregano
½ teaspoon dried mint
Salt and black pepper to taste

Toss the peppers, onion, cucumber, broccoli, and olives in a bowl. In a separate bowl, whisk together the dressing ingredients. Taste for seasoning. Arrange the tomatoes and feta in a bowl or platter, then add the other vegetables. Pour the dressing over the salad and toss well.

Potato Salad 1

SERVES 6

This is my husband's favorite potato salad. His mother has made it for all their family picnics over many years, and this simple, all-American recipe is still a big hit. My mother-in-law occasionally serves it warm for dinner. She prepares it while the potatoes are still hot.

5 large potatoes, peeled and cut into ½-inch slices
4 ribs of celery, minced
½ small yellow onion, minced
1 cup low-fat mayonnaise
  Salt to taste
½ teaspoon black pepper

Cook the potatoes in boiling water until just tender (about 15 minutes), then drain. Cool slightly, then chill in the refrigerator for at least 30 minutes. Combine with the remaining ingredients. Taste for seasoning.

Potato Salad II

SERVES 6

This is a delicious dairy-free potato salad. I sometimes add steamed broccoli and carrots for extra nutrition.

    5 large red potatoes, unpeeled, cut in half lengthwise and then into 1-inch
        slices
    1 small red onion, sliced into ¼-inch rings
    2 tablespoons capers, rinsed
    ¼ cup sliced black olives
    ½ bunch parsley, chopped
    ¼ cup olive oil
      Juice of 1 lemon
    2 tablespoons white wine
      Salt to taste
    ½ teaspoon black pepper
    1 teaspoon dried dill weed

Cook the potatoes in boiling water about 15 minutes, just until tender. Drain. Turn them into a bowl and add the remaining ingredients. Toss gently. Taste for seasoning.

Vegetable Slaw

SERVES 6

I've always enjoyed a homemade vegetable slaw. It's excellent as part of a cold salad plate or as an accompaniment to a sandwich for lunch. And, of course, it is the quintessential picnic salad. Into the bargain, it turns out that cabbage and carrots come highly recommended by the American Cancer Society.

1 small head cabbage, finely chopped
1 medium carrot, shredded
½ small red onion, minced

Dressing:

1 cup cholesterol-free mayonnaise
3 tablespoons cider vinegar
1 tablespoon Dijon mustard
1 tablespoon dried dill weed
1 cup buttermilk or soy milk
Salt to taste
½ teaspoon white pepper

In a large bowl, toss together the cabbage, carrot, and onion. In a separate bowl, combine the dressing ingredients and whisk until smooth. Pour over the vegetables and toss well. Taste for seasoning.

Panzanella

SERVES 4

Enjoy this delicious salad when local tomatoes are in season. If you can't wait until then, buy good vine-ripened hothouse tomatoes. Hard day-old bread is perfect for this dish.

  4 large tomatoes
  8 thick slices hard Italian or French bread, cut or torn into 1-inch cubes
  1 small yellow onion, sliced into thin rings
 10 large leaves fresh basil, chopped
  5 tablespoons extra-virgin olive oil
    Salt to taste
  1 teaspoon black pepper

Cut the tomatoes in half lengthwise, then slice each half into 5 or 6 wedges. Place the tomatoes and any juices in a mixing bowl. Add the bread, onion, and basil and toss. Sprinkle with the olive oil, salt, and pepper. Toss well. Taste for seasoning.

Black Bean Salad (Oil-Free)

SERVES 6

You won't miss the oil in this healthful, flavorful salad.

1 pound black beans, picked over
  Corn kernels cut from 5 ears, or 2 cups frozen kernels
1 small red onion, minced
2 large ripe tomatoes, diced
4 small carrots, diced
  Freshly grated zest of 1 lemon
  Juice of 2 lemons
2 teaspoons chili powder
  Salt to taste
1 teaspoon black pepper

Cook the beans according to the package directions. Rinse under cold water, drain, put in a large bowl, and set aside. Cook the corn in boiling water for 3 minutes, drain, and add to the cooked beans. Add the remaining ingredients and toss well. Taste for seasoning.

Dijon Pasta Salad

SERVES 8

Our customers love this healthful mélange. We have Lynne, a former manager, to thank for the combination.

1 pound tricolor rotini or fusilli
3 small bell peppers, 1 red, 1 yellow, and 1 green, seeded and cut into ¼-inch ribs
½ cup olive oil plus 1 teaspoon
½ large bunch broccoli, bottom 1 inch of stems removed and discarded
1 small red onion, sliced into ¼-inch rings and separated
4 large cloves garlic, minced
⅔ cup Dijon mustard
3 tablespoons red-wine vinegar
1 tablespoon dried tarragon
Salt to taste
1 teaspoon black pepper

Cook the pasta according to the package directions. Add the sliced peppers to the boiling pasta during the last minute of cooking time. Drain and run under cold water to stop the cooking. Drain again and turn into a large bowl. Toss with 1 teaspoon of the olive oil and set aside. Slice the broccoli stems on the diagonal, ¼ inch thick, and chop the florets into small pieces and add to the pasta. Add the onion, garlic, ½ cup olive oil, mustard, vinegar, tarragon, salt, and pepper. Toss well. Taste for seasoning.

Swiss Pasta Salad

SERVES 8

This colorful salad is especially popular at dinner, teamed with a light soup.

        1 pound rigatoni, ziti, or penne
        ½ cup olive oil plus 1 teaspoon
        1 bunch broccoli, bottom 1 inch of stems removed and discarded
        4 carrots, julienned
    One 10-ounce bag fresh spinach, chopped
        8 ounces Swiss cheese, diced
        2 cloves garlic, minced
        Juice of 2 lemons
        2 teaspoons dried dill weed
        1 teaspoon dried tarragon
        Salt to taste
        ½ teaspoon black pepper

Cook the pasta according to the package directions. Rinse under cold water and drain. Place in a bowl and toss with 1 teaspoon of the olive oil. Slice the broccoli stems on the diagonal, ¼-inch thick, and chop the florets into small pieces and add to the pasta. Add the remaining ingredients and toss. Taste for seasoning.

Oriental Linguine Salad

SERVES 6

We have been preparing this healthful salad for more than a decade and our customers still enjoy it so much that we make it nearly every day. You can stir-fry any of your favorite vegetables and toss in nuts or sesame seeds for variety.

 1 pound linguine
 1 teaspoon olive oil
½ cup sesame or soybean oil
 4 cloves garlic, chopped
 1-inch piece fresh ginger, peeled and minced, or 1 teaspoon ground ginger
½ teaspoon crushed red pepper flakes, or to taste
 1 bunch broccoli, bottom 1 inch of stems removed and discarded, chopped
 4 carrots, peeled and cut on the diagonal into ¼-inch slices
½ bunch celery, cut on the diagonal into ¼-inch slices
¼ cup walnut halves
½ cup tamari or soy sauce
 2 tablespoons honey
 1 teaspoon black pepper

Cook the linguine according to the package directions. Drain, run under cold water, drain again, then toss with the olive oil to prevent sticking. Set aside. Heat the sesame or soybean oil in a large skillet over medium heat and add the garlic, ginger, and red pepper flakes. Cook, stirring frequently, for 1 minute. Add the broccoli stems, carrots, celery, and walnuts. Raise the heat to high and cook uncovered for 3 to 5 minutes, stirring frequently, until the vegetables are crisp-tender. Stir in the broccoli florets, tamari or soy sauce, honey, and pepper. Continue cooking and stirring for 1 minute.

Pour over the linguine and toss well, using two wooden spoons. Taste for seasoning.

Greek Pasta Salad

SERVES 8

This salad is so popular at **Claire's** that we added it to our permanent menu and make it every day.

1 pound bow ties, ziti, or penne
½ cup olive oil plus 1 teaspoon
3 peppers, 1 each red, yellow, and green, sliced into thin ribs
1 bunch broccoli, bottom 1 inch of stems removed and discarded, chopped
1 English (seedless) cucumber, cut in half lengthwise and chopped
8 ounces Greek olives
1 small red onion, sliced into thin rings
2 tomatoes, cut in half, then into wedges
8 ounces feta cheese, diced
2 cloves garlic, minced
   Juice of 2 lemons
2 tablespoons red-wine vinegar
¼ teaspoon dried mint
¼ teaspoon dried oregano
   Salt and black pepper to taste

Cook the pasta according to the package directions. Rinse under cold water, drain, turn into a bowl, and toss with 1 teaspoon of the olive oil. Add the remaining ingredients and toss well. Taste for seasoning.

Pasta Cohen

SERVES 8

This delicious "smoky" pasta salad gets its name from Don Cohen, a former promotions director at New Haven's Channel 8, who arranged for us to cater a press conference there. I named this salad after him because he deserved a special place on our menu for all his good advice and kind words.

    1 pound penne or bow ties
One 10-ounce box frozen green peas
    1 tablespoon olive oil
    1 small red onion, sliced into thin rings
    2 tablespoons capers, rinsed
    ¼ cup sliced black olives
    8 ounces smoked mozzarella, chopped

Dressing:

    1 cup milk
    4 scallions, white plus 3 inches of green, chopped
    ½ bunch parsley, chopped
    1 cup low-fat mayonnaise
    1 tablespoon dried dill weed
      Salt to taste
    1 teaspoon black pepper

Cook the pasta according to the package directions. Add the frozen peas to the cooking pasta just before draining. Drain, run under cold water to stop the cooking, drain again, turn into a large bowl, and toss with the olive oil. Add the onion, capers, olives, and mozzarella and toss.

Place the milk, scallions, and parsley in a blender. Cover and blend on high speed for 15 seconds. Pour into bowl. Add the mayonnaise, dill weed, salt, and pepper. Whisk well. Taste for seasoning. Pour the dressing over the pasta salad and toss well. Taste again for seasoning.

Summer Pasta Salad

SERVES 8

This is a terrific salad to make when fresh corn and tomatoes are plentiful.

1 pound pasta elbows
  Corn kernels cut from 5 ears, or 2 cups frozen kernels
2 cups cooked or canned chickpeas
½ small red onion, diced
¼ cup chopped walnuts
3 large ripe tomatoes, cut into ½-inch pieces

Dressing:

1 cup milk
1 cup chopped parsley
2 cloves garlic, chopped
½ small red onion, chopped
1 cup low-fat mayonnaise
1 tablespoon dried dill weed
  Salt to taste
1 teaspoon black pepper

Cook the pasta according to the package directions. Add the corn to the pasta during the last 3 minutes of cooking time. Drain, run under cold water to stop the cooking, drain again, and turn into a large bowl. Add the chickpeas, onion, walnuts, and tomatoes. Toss gently and set aside.

Into a blender, put the milk, parsley, garlic, and onion. Blend on high speed for 15 seconds. Pour into a bowl. Add the mayonnaise, dill weed, salt, and pepper. Whisk until smooth. Taste for seasoning.

Pour the dressing over the pasta salad and toss well. Taste again for seasoning.

Curried Pasta Salad

SERVES 8

You'll love the flavors of curry, chutney, and tart apples in this dish.

> 1 pound medium pasta shells
> 1 bunch broccoli, bottom 1 inch of stems removed and discarded
> One 10-ounce box frozen green peas
> 4 medium carrots, sliced on the diagonal into ¼-inch pieces
> 1 small red onion, chopped
> 2 large cloves garlic, minced
> 2 Granny Smith apples, diced
> ½ cup plus 2 tablespoons olive oil
> 1 tablespoon curry powder
> ½ cup bottled mango chutney (found in the condiment section of most supermarkets)
> Salt to taste
> Pinch cayenne pepper
> ½ teaspoon black pepper

Cook the pasta according to the package directions. Meanwhile, separate the broccoli stems from the florets. Slice the stems into ¼-inch pieces and set aside. Chop the florets into small pieces and set aside. Add the peas, carrots, and broccoli stems to the pasta during the last minute of cooking. Add the broccoli florets just before draining. Drain, rinse under cold water to stop the cooking, then drain again and turn into a large bowl. Add the onion, garlic, apples, olive oil, curry powder, chutney, salt, cayenne, and pepper. Toss well. Taste for seasoning.

Mexican Pasta Salad

SERVES 8

The creamy salsa dressing is sensational on this colorful salad.

1 pound rigatoni
Corn kernels cut from 3 ears, or one 10-ounce box frozen kernels
1 small red onion, sliced into ¼-inch rings and separated
3 bell peppers, 1 red, 1 yellow, and 1 green, seeded and diced
2 tablespoons chopped parsley
¼ cup sliced black olives
2 teaspoons chili powder
1½ cups Salsa, preferably homemade (see page 164)
½ cup low-fat sour cream
Salt to taste
1 teaspoon black pepper

Cook the pasta according to the package directions. Add the corn to the pasta during the last 3 minutes of cooking time. Drain, run under cold water to stop the cooking, then drain again and turn into a large bowl. Add the remaining ingredients and toss well. Taste for seasoning.

Mediterranean Rice Salad

SERVES 8

This is a beautiful salad, colorful and delicious.

    4 cups brown rice
10 cups water
  1 small red onion, finely chopped
One 10-ounce bag fresh spinach, cleaned and chopped
  8 ounces feta cheese, crumbled
16 oil-cured black olives, pitted and chopped
  1 tablespoon capers, rinsed
  3 tomatoes, diced
¼ cup olive oil
   Juice of 2 lemons
¼ teaspoon dried mint
¼ teaspoon dried oregano
½ teaspoon black pepper
   Salt to taste

Put the rice and water in a large pot. Cover and bring to a boil over high heat. Lower the heat and simmer, covered, for 30 to 45 minutes, until the rice is tender and the water is absorbed. Turn into a large bowl and fluff with a fork. Add the remaining ingredients and toss well. Taste for seasoning. Serve warm or chilled.

Pasta Salad with Broccoli and Potatoes

SERVES 8

This is terrific to take along on a picnic. It keeps well and is full of healthful vegetables.

1 pound penne
½ cup plus 1 tablespoon olive oil
3 large potatoes, cut into ¾-inch pieces
1 bunch broccoli, bottom 1 inch of stems removed and discarded
3 large cloves garlic, minced
Juice of 2 lemons
Salt to taste
1 teaspoon black pepper

Cook the pasta according to the package directions. Drain and rinse under cold water to stop the cooking, drain again, and toss with 1 tablespoon of the olive oil to prevent sticking. Set aside. Bring a large pot of water to a boil. Add the potatoes and a little salt. Cook about 10 minutes, until crisp-tender. Meanwhile, separate the broccoli stems from the florets. Cut the stems into ¼-inch pieces. Cut the florets into small pieces. When the potatoes are crisp-tender, add the broccoli stems and cook for 2 minutes more, or until the potatoes are just tender. Add the florets and cook for 30 seconds.

Drain, run under cold water, and drain again. Add to the pasta. Add the garlic and toss well. Add the remaining ½ cup olive oil, lemon juice, salt, and pepper and toss well again. Taste for seasoning.

Green Bean Salad

SERVES 4

Green beans, or string beans as my mom calls them, were a part of many spring and summer meals during my childhood. I have clear memories of Mom sitting at the kitchen table snapping off the tips of the beans while chatting with one of the neighbors, who often visited for an afternoon cup of coffee.

1 pound green beans
1 medium onion, sliced into thin rings
¼ cup olive oil
3 tablespoons red-wine vinegar
   Salt to taste
1 teaspoon black pepper
¼ cup chopped fresh basil or ½ teaspoon dried basil
½ teaspoon dried oregano

Snap or cut off the stem end of the beans, then snap or cut into halves or thirds. Bring water to a boil in a large covered pot. Add the green beans and boil for 3 to 5 minutes, until crisp-tender. Drain, run under cold water, then drain again. Turn into a bowl, add the remaining ingredients, and toss. Taste for seasoning.

Angel-Hair Pasta Salad

SERVES 8

This is one of the prettiest salads we make at **Claire's**. It contains tiny pieces of colorful vegetables tossed with long, thin pasta. It's a big hit at the restaurant, and on our family picnics as well.

    1 pound angel-hair pasta
    ½ cup extra-virgin olive oil plus 1 teaspoon
    1 small zucchini, diced
    2 medium carrots, diced
    1 small yellow squash, diced
    1 small red onion, diced
    3 cups diced broccoli florets
    1 tomato, diced
    1 small yellow bell pepper, seeded and diced
    1 small red bell pepper, seeded and diced
    2 cloves garlic, minced
      Freshly grated zest of 1 lemon
      Juice of 2 lemons
    1 tablespoon dried dill weed
      Salt to taste
    2 teaspoons black pepper

Cook the pasta according to the package directions. Drain, rinse under cold water, drain again, and turn into a large bowl. Toss with 1 teaspoon of the olive oil. Add the diced vegetables to the pasta and toss. In a separate bowl, whisk together the ½ cup olive oil, lemon zest and juice, dill weed, salt, and pepper. Taste for seasoning.

Pour the dressing over the pasta and vegetables and toss well. Serve immediately or cover and refrigerate. Toss again just before serving.

My Mom's Dinner Salad

SERVES 6

This was the tossed salad Mom served *every* night with dinner for many years. We always loved the fresh lemon taste. She now tries out different dressings, but this salad remains a favorite.

    1 small head iceberg lettuce
    2 cloves garlic, minced
    ¼ cup olive oil
      Juice of 1 lemon
      Salt to taste
    1 teaspoon black pepper (optional)

Tear the washed and drained lettuce into a large bowl. Sprinkle the garlic over the top. Pour the oil over the salad and toss. Squeeze the lemon over the top. Sprinkle with salt, and pepper if desired. Toss well. Taste for seasoning.

Carrot-Raisin Salad (Oil-Free)

SERVES 4

This colorful salad is sweet and crunchy.

    8 carrots, coarsely grated
    ½ cup golden raisins
    ½ cup chopped walnuts
    ¼ cup raspberry vinegar
    ¼ teaspoon ground ginger
      Salt to taste
    ½ teaspoon white pepper

Combine all the ingredients in a bowl and toss well. Taste for seasoning.

Gazpacho Salad

SERVES 4

You'll enjoy this salad version of our terrific gazpacho soup.

½ English (seedless) cucumber
1 small red bell pepper, seeded
1 small green bell pepper, seeded
1 small red onion
1 large tomato
¼ cup chopped flat-leaf parsley
2 cloves garlic, minced
3 tablespoons extra-virgin olive oil
  Juice of 1 lemon
2 tablespoons red-wine vinegar
2 shakes Tabasco
  Salt to taste
1 teaspoon black pepper
2 tablespoons plain bread crumbs

Chop the cucumber, peppers, onion, and tomato into ½-inch pieces and place in a large bowl with any juices. Toss. Add the parsley, garlic, olive oil, lemon juice, vinegar, and Tabasco. Toss well. Sprinkle with the salt, pepper, and bread crumbs and toss well again. Taste for seasoning.

Orzo Salad

SERVES 8

Orzo is a tiny rice-shaped pasta that makes a good alternative to rice. You'll enjoy it in soups or salads, or any dish that calls for rice.

1 pound orzo
1 medium zucchini, diced
1 medium yellow squash, diced
¼ pound snow peas
½ cup canola oil
2 tablespoons tamari or soy sauce
½ teaspoon ground ginger
½ teaspoon black pepper
  Salt to taste

Cook the orzo according to the package directions. Add the zucchini, yellow squash, and snow peas during the last 3 minutes of cooking. Drain, rinse under cold water, drain again, and turn into a large bowl. Add the canola oil, tamari or soy sauce, ginger, pepper, and salt. Toss well. Taste for seasoning.

My Favorite Tossed Salad

SERVES 4

This salad has a great variety of flavors: sweet, bitter, fruity, mild, and strong. I hope it will become your favorite too.

1 head Bibb lettuce, torn into 2-inch lengths
1 bunch arugula, cut into 2-inch lengths
1 small head radicchio, chopped
1 small head endive, sliced into ¼-inch rings
¼ cup extra-virgin olive oil
3 tablespoons raspberry vinegar
Salt to taste
½ teaspoon black pepper

Place the lettuce, arugula, radicchio, and endive in a large bowl and toss. Add the oil, vinegar, salt, and pepper and toss again. Taste for seasoning.

Dandelion Salad

SERVES 4

My grandmother made this salad all summer long. She used the dandelions that grew on her lawn. Today, many Italian markets carry dandelion leaves during late spring and summer. They are delicious in this salad or in minestrone in place of or in addition to spinach.

    30 to 40 dandelion stems, torn into bite-sized pieces
    ¼ cup extra-virgin olive oil
        Juice of 1 lemon
        Salt to taste
    1 teaspoon black pepper

Place the torn dandelion leaves in a large bowl. Add the oil and toss to coat well. Add the lemon juice, salt, and pepper and toss well again. Taste for seasoning.

Broccoli Salad

SERVES 6

Broccoli was always popular at our house. My mother served this dish with our dinner at least once a week. We never tired of it. In fact, we still look forward to this tasty and healthful broccoli salad each Sunday at our family dinner.

1 bunch broccoli, bottom 1 inch of stems removed and discarded
4 large cloves garlic, minced
3 tablespoons olive oil
   Juice of 1 lemon
   Salt to taste
1 teaspoon black pepper

Separate the broccoli stems and florets. Slice the stems on the diagonal into ⅓-inch pieces. Cut the florets into medium pieces. Set aside. Cook the stems in boiling water for 3 minutes, then add the florets and cook for an additional minute, until crisp-tender. Drain, run under cold water to stop the cooking, drain again, and turn into a bowl. Add the garlic, olive oil, lemon juice, salt, and pepper. Toss well. Taste for seasoning.

Corn Salad

SERVES 4

Enjoy this bright salad when corn is in season. Always cook your corn as soon as possible after it is picked.

    6 ears corn
    1 carrot, scrubbed and diced
    1 small red bell pepper, seeded and diced
    1 large, ripe tomato, chopped
    ½ small red onion, minced

Dressing:

    3 tablespoons olive oil
     Juice of 1 lime
    1 teaspoon chili powder
     Salt to taste
    1 teaspoon black pepper

Bring water to a boil in a large covered pot. Meanwhile, cut the corn kernels from the ears. Cook the corn in the boiling water for 2 minutes. Add the carrot and cook 1 minute. Drain, run under cold water, drain again, and turn into a bowl. Add the bell pepper, tomato, and onion and toss. In a separate bowl, whisk together the dressing ingredients. Taste for seasoning. Pour over the salad and toss.

Beet Salad

SERVES 6

Claire's prepared the food for a press conference when the Russian Circus visited New Haven in 1989. I thought it would be fun to make borscht and black bread. I peeled two cases of fresh beets, and my hands were a lovely purple for days. I had refused to peel a beet since, until I tested this recipe. Then I remembered just how wonderful fresh beets are.

  6 large fresh beets, peeled
  1 Spanish onion, sliced into ⅛-inch rings
  3 tablespoons olive oil
  2 tablespoons red-wine vinegar
    Salt to taste
  ¼ teaspoon black pepper

Bring 4 quarts of water to a boil in a large covered pot. Add the beets. Cook until they are tender when pierced with a fork, about 10 minutes. Drain. When they are cool enough to handle, slice the beets into ¼-inch rounds. Place in a bowl. Add the remaining ingredients and toss gently. Taste for seasoning. Serve at room temperature or chilled.

Pasta Salad Sharon

SERVES 8

One gray and rainy day at **Claire's,** Eileen, one of the cheeriest employees we've ever had the pleasure to work with, was feeling down. I invited Eileen into the kitchen to invent a new pasta salad, since there's nothing like cooking or baking something beautiful to give your mind a break from a problem. Eileen and I worked together and came up with this delicious salad, and she named it for her sister Sharon. My mom was right once again: food is the best medicine.

    1 pound tricolor fusilli
    1 tablespoon olive oil
    1 large head escarole, chopped
    2 carrots, scrubbed and julienned
    ½ small red cabbage, cut into 1-inch pieces
    6 sun-dried tomatoes, cut into thin strips

Dressing:

    ½ cup olive oil
    ½ cup chopped fresh basil
    2 tablespoons grated Parmesan
    1 teaspoon black pepper
    4 large cloves garlic, chopped
      Salt to taste

Cook the pasta according to the package directions. Drain, run under cold water, drain again, turn into a large bowl, and toss with the 1 tablespoon olive oil to prevent sticking. Set aside.

Bring a large pot of water to a boil. Add the escarole and cook 5 minutes, until crisp-tender. Using a slotted spoon, remove the escarole to a colander to drain. Set aside to drain.

Add the carrots to the boiling water. Cook 2 minutes, until crisp-tender. Using a slotted spoon, remove the carrots to the colander containing the escarole.

Add the cabbage and sun-dried tomatoes to the boiling water. Cook for 2 minutes, until the cabbage is crisp-tender. Drain the cabbage and sun-dried tomatoes, run them under cold water, and drain again.

Place all the dressing ingredients in a blender. Blend on high speed for 30 seconds, or until smooth. Taste for seasoning.

Add the vegetables to the pasta and toss well. Pour the dressing over the salad and toss well. Taste for seasoning.

Cucumber Salad

SERVES 4

This is a light and refreshing salad, perfect for hot summer days.

- 1 large English (seedless) cucumber, sliced into ¼-inch rounds
- 1 small white onion, sliced into thin rings
- 3 tablespoons olive oil
- 2 tablespoons white vinegar
  - Juice of 1 lemon
- 1 tablespoon dried dill weed
  - Salt to taste
- 1 teaspoon black pepper

Place the cucumber and onion in a bowl and toss. Pour the olive oil over the top and toss well. Add the remaining ingredients and toss well. Taste for seasoning.

Dressings

Salad dressing is as important as the sauce on the pasta, the maple syrup on the French toast, the fresh berries on the angel food cake. Its flavors should wake up your ingredients, not overpower them. You don't need a complicated dressing for each salad; sometimes crisp romaine leaves tossed with slivers of fresh garlic, a little extra-virgin olive oil, salt, and black pepper are perfect with dinner.

Again, I encourage you to experiment, using high-quality oils and vinegars instead of store-bought dressings. Almost all packaged dressings contain preservatives and sugar—and they just don't taste very good!

Store your dressings in jars or Tupperware-type covered bowls in your refrigerator. Buy pretty dressing servers and you'll be all set. I have been spoiled by homemade dressings. You will be too.

Creamy Italian Dressing

MAKES ABOUT 1½ PINTS

We use this dressing for salads, as a sandwich spread, and as a dip for vegetables. We recommend it for the parties we cater because the rich flavor appeals to so many.

  1 cup low-fat sour cream
  1 cup low-fat mayonnaise
  ⅔ cup buttermilk, plus extra for thinning
  2 tablespoons red-wine vinegar
  ¼ cup olive oil
  4 cloves garlic, minced
  2 teaspoons dried oregano
  2 teaspoons dried basil
    Salt and black pepper to taste

Measure all the ingredients into a bowl and whisk well. Whisk in additional buttermilk, 2 tablespoons at a time, until the desired consistency is reached. Taste for seasoning.

Creamy Romano-Dill Dressing

MAKES ABOUT 1 PINT

This is another luscious salad dressing, rich and creamy and immensely popular at **Claire's**.

1 cup low-fat mayonnaise
⅔ cup buttermilk
¼ cup grated Romano
4 large cloves garlic, minced
1 tablespoon dried dill weed
1 teaspoon black pepper
  Salt to taste

Measure all the ingredients into a bowl and whisk well. Taste for seasoning.

Herbal Vinaigrette Dressing

MAKES ABOUT 1 PINT

This dressing is perfect for tossed green salads, pasta salads, and potato or other vegetable salads.

1 cup olive oil
⅓ cup red-wine vinegar
  Juice of 2 lemons
  Salt to taste
1 teaspoon black pepper
2 teaspoons each dried basil, oregano, and tarragon
1 tablespoon Dijon mustard
1 tablespoon soy sauce

Combine all the ingredients in a bowl. Whisk well. Taste for seasoning.

Creamy Scallion Dill Dressing

MAKES ABOUT 1 PINT

This is the dressing we use for our Pasta Cohen (see page 96), as well as for many other salads. It's great with steamed green beans, slices of red onions, and wedges of ripe, red tomatoes.

     1 cup milk
     ½ bunch parsley, chopped
     4 scallions, white plus 3 inches of green, chopped
     1 cup low-fat mayonnaise
     1 tablespoon dried dill weed
       Salt to taste
     1 teaspoon black pepper

Into a blender, put the milk, parsley, and scallions. Cover and blend on high speed for 15 seconds. Pour into a bowl. Add the mayonnaise, dill weed, salt, and pepper. Whisk together until well blended. Taste for seasoning.

Salt-Free Yogurt Dressing

MAKES ABOUT 1 PINT

This fat-free dressing has a delicious, fresh taste. Try it as the dressing for a potato salad or as a dip for carrot sticks.

    1 pint plain nonfat yogurt
    2 teaspoons freshly grated lime zest
      Juice of 1 lime
    ¼ teaspoon ground ginger
    1 teaspoon dried dill weed
      Black pepper to taste

Put all the ingredients in a bowl and whisk well. Taste for seasoning.

Mustard-Tarragon Dressing

MAKES ABOUT 1 PINT

I love this dressing on a vegetable salad, tossed with a pasta salad, as a sandwich spread, and as a dip for vegetables. It's so good, some of our customers ask for an extra serving to spread on their bread in place of butter.

    1 cup cholesterol-free mayonnaise
    ½ cup Dijon mustard
    2 teaspoons dried tarragon
    2 teaspoons white vinegar
    ½ cup buttermilk
      Salt and black pepper to taste

Measure all the ingredients into a bowl and whisk well. Taste for seasoning.

Tahini Dressing

MAKES ABOUT 1 PINT

We have always served this creamy, garlicky dressing on our pita bread sandwiches at **Claire's**. It's delicious, high in protein, and free of dairy products. Many of our customers order tahini on their tossed salads as well, and we recommend tahini dressing for our tabouli and falafel salads.

    1 cup cold water
    5 large cloves garlic, minced
      Juice of 1 lemon
    ½ cup chopped parsley
    1 cup tahini (sesame paste; found in health-food stores)
      Salt to taste
    1 teaspoon black pepper

Put all the ingredients into a blender. Cover and blend on high speed for 30 seconds, until smooth. Taste for seasoning.

Tomato-Basil Dressing

MAKES ABOUT 1 PINT

This delicious cholesterol-free dressing is marvelous over a tossed green salad, potato salad, or pasta salad. We sometimes add a little to our pesto pasta, and it's terrific.

    1½ cups olive oil
    1 large ripe tomato, chopped, with juice
    1 bunch fresh basil, chopped
    ¼ cup chopped parsley
    Salt to taste
    1 teaspoon black pepper

Put the ingredients into a blender, cover, and blend on high speed for 30 seconds. Taste for seasoning.

My Mom's Olive Oil and Lemon Dressing

MAKES ABOUT 1 CUP

I love this plain and simple dressing. Mom uses so many lemons at home that she buys them by the dozen.

    ¾ cup olive oil
    Juice of 3 lemons
    4 large cloves garlic, minced
    Salt and black pepper to taste

Combine the ingredients in a jar and shake well. Taste for seasoning.

Basil Vinaigrette

MAKES ABOUT 1 PINT

Toward the end of our summer, my neighbor Jane brings me bagfuls of basil from her garden. We're very grateful for this gift, and put it to delicious use. We gladly make basil pesto and basil sauces, add basil leaves to our salads, and prepare vats of this savory dressing for our salads.

    1¾ cups olive oil
    1 large bunch basil, leaves and thin stems chopped
       Juice of 1 lemon
       Salt to taste
    1 teaspoon black pepper

Combine the ingredients in a blender, cover, and blend on medium speed for 15 seconds. Scrape down the sides, using a rubber spatula, then blend on high speed for 15 seconds, until smooth. Taste for seasoning.

Sun-Dried Tomato Vinaigrette

MAKES ABOUT 1 PINT

Our customers love sun-dried tomatoes in pasta salads, sauces, and pestos, and in this dressing, which is very versatile. At home, I use it to baste vegetable kebobs and veggie burgers for grilling.

1½ cups olive oil
¼ cup oil-packed sun-dried tomatoes (found in the gourmet food section of most supermarkets)
2 tablespoons white vinegar
Salt and black pepper to taste

Put the ingredients in a blender, cover, and blend on high speed for 15 seconds. Taste for seasoning.

Raspberry Vinaigrette

MAKES ABOUT 1 PINT

I first made this dressing for the tossed salad I brought to a cookout at the home of my good friend Claudia. Many people asked for the recipe. After that I added the dressing to the menu at **Claire's,** and it was a big hit.

1¼ cups olive oil
¾ cup raspberry vinegar
Freshly grated zest of 1 lime
Juice of 2 limes
1 teaspoon ground ginger
Salt to taste
½ teaspoon white pepper

Put all the ingredients in a bowl and whisk well. Taste for seasoning.

Pasta and Sauces

This chapter will provide you with ideas for many delicious dinners. Most sauces can be prepared in advance and refrigerated or frozen after they have been cooled to room temperature, and then can be slowly reheated when needed. Specific pasta shapes have been suggested in many of the recipes, but they are only suggestions and personal favorites. While I would love to use only fresh local tomatoes for our tomato sauces, I don't usually have that luxury, given the short growing season in New England. Canned tomatoes are different, but still very good; look for cans that say "Imported from Italy," not just "Italian-style." There really is a difference in flavor. Expect to pay more for these tomatoes; they're well worth the extra cost.

Marinara Sauce

SERVES 6

There's nothing quite like a simple marinara. The delightful aroma will fill your kitchen, tempting all who enter. This wonderful sauce is quick and easy to make, requiring only staple ingredients and allowing you to offer last-minute dinner invitations to your friends. Invite them back to the house after a day at the beach or an evening of theater. Put your water for pasta on to boil while you prepare this delicious sauce and make a simple salad, and within the hour you and some very grateful friends will be enjoying a lovely meal.

½ cup olive oil
6 large cloves garlic, minced
Two 28-ounce cans whole peeled San Marzano tomatoes (found in Italian import stores, or substitute another good Italian tomato)
½ cup chopped fresh basil
1 teaspoon crushed red pepper flakes
Salt to taste
Black pepper to taste
1 pound penne, or pasta of your choice

Heat the oil in a large skillet over low heat. Add the garlic and cook for 3 minutes, stirring frequently, until golden brown. Do not let the garlic burn or your sauce will be bitter. Add the tomatoes and raise the heat to medium. Simmer for 10 minutes, stirring often. Using a spoon, break up the tomatoes into small pieces. Add the basil, red pepper flakes, salt, and pepper. Simmer, stirring frequently, for another 15 to 20 minutes, until the sauce is thick. Taste for seasonings.

Meanwhile, bring water for cooking the pasta to a boil. Cook the pasta according to the package directions. Drain and turn into a serving bowl. Add a little cooked marinara sauce to the pasta and toss well. Spoon the remaining marinara over the top. Grind additional black pepper over the top if desired. Serve with thick slices of good bread for dunking.

Pomodoro (Fresh Tomato) Sauce

SERVES 6

We prepare this marvelous sauce of fresh tomatoes only during the summer months, when native tomatoes are beautiful and plentiful. The sauce cooks fast, so I put water on to boil for the pasta before I begin the sauce.

- ½ cup extra-virgin olive oil
- 6 large cloves garlic, chopped
- 8 large ripe tomatoes, each cut into 16 wedges, with juices
- ½ cup chopped fresh basil
- Salt to taste
- 1 teaspoon black pepper
- 1 pound angel-hair pasta or other pasta

Heat the oil in a large skillet over low heat. Add the garlic and cook, stirring frequently, for 3 minutes, until golden brown. Do not let the garlic burn or your sauce will be bitter. Add the tomatoes and their juices, basil, salt, and pepper. Raise the heat to medium and cover. Simmer the sauce for 10 minutes, stirring frequently, until the tomatoes are soft. Remove the cover and continue simmering for 15 minutes, until the sauce thickens slightly. Taste for seasoning.

Cook the pasta according to the package directions. Drain and turn into a serving bowl. Spoon a little sauce over the top and toss well. Spoon the remaining sauce over the top. Pass the pepper grinder and freshly grated Romano if you wish.

Sicilian Sauce 1

SERVES 6

This is my interpretation of the wonderful chunky sauce my paternal grand-mother made for my brother Billy and me every year during our summer visit to her home. She was a marvelous cook. We were her only grandchildren for many years, so she and her glorious recipes were all ours. Fresh fettuccine has always been a favorite for me; Grandma made tender, perfect noodles. This sauce came from her childhood in Sicily, and she spooned plenty of it over a huge platter of her fresh fettuccine. We always found room for second helpings.

½ cup plus 2 tablespoons olive oil
6 large cloves garlic, chopped
2 small to medium eggplants, chopped
¼ cup water
2 tablespoons capers, rinsed
¼ cup sliced black olives
¼ to ½ teaspoon crushed red pepper flakes
½ teaspoon dried oregano
Two 28-ounce cans Italian whole peeled tomatoes, crushed with your hands
½ cup chopped flat-leaf parsley
Salt to taste
1 teaspoon black pepper
¼ cup chopped fresh basil
1 pound fettuccine, rigatoni, or linguine

Heat the oil in a heavy pot over low heat. Add the garlic and eggplant. Cook for 10 minutes, stirring frequently. Add the water, capers, olives, red pepper flakes, and oregano. Cover, bring to a low boil, and cook for 15 minutes, stirring frequently. Add the tomatoes, parsley, salt, pepper, and basil. Simmer uncovered about 40 minutes, stirring frequently, until the eggplant is tender and the sauce is thick. Taste for seasoning.

Cook the pasta according to the package directions. Drain and turn into a serving bowl. Spoon a little sauce over the top and toss to coat the pasta. Spoon the remaining sauce over the top.

Sicilian Sauce II

SERVES 6

This sauce is hot and spicy. You can adjust the fire by cutting back on the hot cherry peppers. Remember to wash your hands immediately after handling hot peppers, or you might burn your eyes if you touch your face.

    ½ cup plus 2 tablespoons olive oil
    6 large cloves garlic, chopped
    1 small red onion, chopped
    1 medium eggplant, chopped
    2 red bell peppers, seeded and chopped
    2 hot cherry peppers (found in the Italian section of the supermarket),
        chopped
    ¼ cup chopped flat-leaf parsley
    ¼ teaspoon dried oregano
    ¼ cup sliced black olives
    2 tablespoons capers, rinsed
      Salt to taste
    1 teaspoon black pepper
    ¼ teaspoon crushed red pepper flakes
 Two 28-ounce cans Italian whole peeled tomatoes, crushed with your hands
    1 pound ziti, penne, or other pasta

Heat the oil in a heavy pot over low heat. Add the garlic, onion, eggplant, bell peppers, and cherry peppers. Cover and cook for 15 minutes, stirring frequently. Add the parsley, oregano, olives, capers, salt, pepper, red pepper flakes, and tomatoes. Raise the heat to medium. Bring to a low boil and simmer uncovered for 40 minutes, stirring frequently, until the eggplant is tender. Taste for seasoning.

Cook the pasta according to the package directions. Drain and turn into a serving bowl. Spoon a little sauce over the top and toss well. Spoon the remaining sauce over the top.

Puttanesca Sauce

SERVES 6

We serve this flavorful sauce over linguine at **Claire's.**

  ½ cup olive oil
  8 large cloves garlic, chopped
  1 cup sliced black olives
  ½ teaspoon crushed red pepper flakes
  3 tablespoons capers, rinsed
  ¼ cup chopped flat-leaf parsley
  ½ teaspoon dried oregano
Two 28-ounce cans Italian whole peeled tomatoes, crushed with your hands
    Salt and black pepper to taste
  1 pound cooked linguine or other pasta

Heat the oil in a large skillet over low heat. Add the garlic, olives, red pepper flakes, capers, parsley, and oregano. Cook for 10 minutes, stirring frequently. Add the tomatoes, salt, and pepper. Raise the heat to medium and simmer, uncovered, for 30 minutes, stirring frequently, until the sauce is thick. Taste for seasoning.

Cook the pasta according to the package directions. Drain and turn into a serving bowl. Spoon a little sauce over the top and toss well. Spoon the remaining sauce over the top.

Piselli Sauce

SERVES 6

If you love green peas and tomatoes you'll love this sauce. We serve it over medium pasta shells, which create little bundles of flavor.

½ cup extra-virgin olive oil
1 medium yellow onion, chopped
6 large cloves garlic, chopped
½ cup chopped flat-leaf parsley
½ teaspoon dried oregano
  Pinch dried rosemary
Two 28-ounce cans Italian whole peeled tomatoes, crushed with your hands
  Salt and black pepper to taste
One 10-ounce box frozen green peas
1 pound medium pasta shells

Heat the oil in a heavy pot over low heat. Add the onion, garlic, parsley, oregano, and rosemary. Cover and cook for 10 minutes, stirring frequently, until the onions are soft. Add the tomatoes, salt, and pepper. Raise the heat to medium, bring to a low boil, and simmer uncovered for 30 minutes, stirring frequently, until the sauce is thickened. Add the peas and continue cooking for 10 minutes, stirring frequently, until the peas are heated through.

Cook the pasta according to the package directions. Drain and turn into a serving bowl. Spoon a little sauce over the top and toss well. Spoon the remaining sauce over the top.

Amatriciana Sauce

SERVES 6

This is our meatless, cholesterol-free version of the pancetta-flavored tomato sauce so many of us enjoyed before the problem of cholesterol was posed. The flavor is rich, and Fakin Bakin has a familiar smoky taste. Prepare this delicious sauce for anyone who loves bacon or pancetta in a sauce but cannot have the cholesterol, and you will make that person very happy.

½ cup olive oil
1 medium yellow onion, chopped
4 large cloves garlic, chopped
One 8-ounce package Fakin Bakin or other bacon substitute, chopped
     (found in most health-food stores)
¼ cup chopped flat-leaf parsley
½ teaspoon crushed red pepper flakes
Two 28-ounce cans Italian whole peeled tomatoes, crushed with your hands
¼ cup chopped fresh basil
  Salt and black pepper to taste
1 pound rigatoni

Heat the oil in a large skillet over low heat. Add the onion, garlic, and "bacon." Cook, stirring occasionally, for 15 minutes, until the "bacon" browns. Add the parsley, red pepper flakes, tomatoes, basil, salt, and pepper. Bring to a boil and simmer for 40 minutes, stirring occasionally, until the sauce is thickened.

Cook the pasta according to the package directions. Drain and turn into a serving bowl. Spoon a little sauce over the top and toss well. Spoon the remaining sauce over the top.

Garden Sauce

SERVES 6

We serve this vegetable sauce over spinach fettuccine, and our customers eat every bit of it—usually by dunking their bread in whatever sauce may be left on the plate.

½ cup olive oil
4 large cloves garlic, chopped
1 small red onion, chopped
1 small carrot, julienned
1 small zucchini, chopped
1 small yellow squash, chopped
½ small bunch broccoli, bottom 1 inch of stems removed and discarded, chopped, stems separated from florets
¼ cup chopped flat-leaf parsley
¼ teaspoon dried rosemary
Two 28-ounce cans Italian whole peeled tomatoes, crushed with your hands
¼ cup chopped fresh basil
Salt and black pepper to taste
1 pound penne or other pasta

Heat the oil in a large pot over low heat. Add the garlic, onion, carrot, zucchini, yellow squash, and broccoli stems. Cook for 15 minutes, stirring frequently, until the carrots and broccoli stems soften. Add the parsley, rosemary, tomatoes, basil, salt, and pepper. Raise the heat to medium and simmer for 25 minutes, stirring frequently, until the carrots and broccoli stems are just tender. Add the broccoli florets and continue cooking for 10 minutes, stirring frequently, until the florets are just tender. Taste for seasoning.

Cook the pasta according to the package directions. Drain and turn into a serving bowl. Spoon a little sauce over the pasta and toss well. Spoon the remaining sauce over the pasta.

Baked Rigatoni with Amalfitan Sauce

SERVES 6

Every family has its way of distinguishing between maternal and paternal grand-parents. We used the cities each resided in to differentiate between ours. "Grandma and Grandpa in New Haven" were from Amalfi, Italy, and this Grandma cooked with more vegetables, fish, beans, and cheese than "Grandma in Bridgeport," who used more meats and pastas. Luckily, both showed their great love for us by spoiling us with our favorite meals during every visit. This luscious sauce was the Sunday sauce at "Grandma in New Haven's." It's still one of my favorites, and I like seeing my customers enjoy it at **Claire's.**

    1 pound rigatoni, cooked according to package directions
    4 cups Marinara Sauce (see page 127), at room temperature or chilled
    4 eggs, lightly beaten
    ¼ cup grated Parmesan
    1 pound low-fat ricotta
    4 ounces shredded low-fat mozzarella
    Salt and black pepper to taste

Preheat the oven to 375 degrees. Put all the ingredients in a large bowl and toss well. Turn into a rectangular glass baking dish sprayed with nonstick cook-ing spray. Bake about 30 minutes, until heated through and lightly browned on top.

Lasagna Primavera

SERVES 8

When my mom was a child, Catholic Church rules prohibited eating meat on Fridays. Today the rule has been relaxed, and Catholics' abstinence from meat is limited to Holy Days and Fridays during Lent. Luckily, my grandmother and my mother sought variety in their diets and created many different meals for those "meatless days." This vegetarian lasagna is a variation of the one I loved as a child. My brothers and I always ate the leftovers, cold, for breakfast, which didn't make Mom very happy, because she preferred we eat a hot breakfast. We liked it cold though.

- 1 pound lasagna noodles
- 1 pound ricotta
- 3 eggs, lightly beaten
- ¼ cup grated Romano
- 1 cup chopped parsley
- ½ teaspoon black pepper
- 2 cups finely chopped fresh spinach
- 3 medium carrots, cut on the diagonal into ½-inch slices and steamed until crisp-tender
- 1 medium zucchini, cut on the diagonal into ½-inch slices and steamed until crisp-tender
- 1 medium yellow squash, cut on the diagonal into ½-inch slices and steamed until crisp-tender
- 4 cups Marinara Sauce (see page 127)
- 4 ounces shredded mozzarella

Preheat the oven to 350 degrees. Cook the lasagna according to the package directions. Meanwhile, mix together the ricotta and eggs. Mix in the Romano, parsley, pepper, and spinach and set aside. Spread a thin layer of Marinara Sauce evenly across the bottom of a rectangular glass baking dish. Place a single layer of lasagna on the bottom of the pan, overlapping the noodles slightly. Arrange all of the carrots over the noodles, overlapping as needed. Spoon ⅓ of the ricotta filling over the carrots and top with one-quarter of the Marinara Sauce.

Arrange another layer of lasagna over the filling, this time in the opposite direction from the first layer, trimming as necessary. This will help it stay together when cut. Repeat for two more layers using the zucchini, yellow squash, remaining ricotta, and Marinara Sauce, on each layer; end with a layer of lasagna with sauce on top. Sprinkle the mozzarella evenly across the top.

This dish can be prepared 1 day in advance: cover with plastic wrap or wax paper and refrigerate. Do not cover with foil or the acid in the Marinara Sauce can cause bits of foil to get into the sauce. When ready to bake, remove the wrapping and bake in a preheated 350-degree oven for 45 minutes. Let stand about 15 minutes before serving.

Pasta e Ceci
(Pasta and Chickpeas)

SERVES 6

We love "ceci" (pronounced "chechee") beans in our family. Even the name has a good sound to us. My brother Paul and his wife, Kim, often call their little daughter Carley their "little ceci bean." You'll find ceci beans tossed in our salads, mashed into a dip, baked with sweet potatoes, cooked in soups, and in this marvelous sauce. We always soak the chickpeas in water overnight in the refrigerator to cut the cooking time of these hard beans.

  1 pound dry ceci beans (chickpeas), picked over and soaked overnight
  4 quarts water
  ½ cup olive oil
  7 cloves garlic, chopped
  ¼ cup chopped flat-leaf parsley
  ½ teaspoon crushed red pepper flakes
  1 teaspoon dried oregano
  4 cloves garlic, chopped
One 10-ounce bag fresh spinach, chopped
    Salt and black pepper to taste
  1 pound linguine

Drain the soaked chickpeas. Put them in a large pot with the water, cover, and bring to a boil over high heat. Lower the heat to medium and add ¼ cup of the olive oil, 3 cloves of the garlic, the parsley, red pepper flakes, and oregano. Cook over medium heat, uncovered, about 2 hours, stirring occasionally, until the chickpeas are very tender. Partially mash the cooked chickpeas in the pot, using a long-handled potato masher. Keep the chickpeas warm.

In a large skillet over low heat, heat the remaining ¼ cup olive oil. Add the 4 remaining cloves of garlic and cook for 2 minutes, stirring occasionally, until the garlic is golden brown. Add the spinach and sprinkle with salt and pepper. Cover, raise the heat to medium-low, and cook about 3 minutes, stirring after 2

minutes, until the spinach is wilted. Pour the spinach mixture into the chickpeas and mix well. Taste for seasoning.

Cook the linguine according to the package directions. Drain and turn into a serving bowl. Spoon about ¼ of the sauce over the top and toss well. Spoon the remaining sauce over the top. Serve with additional freshly ground black pepper if desired.

Mushrooms Fra Diavolo

SERVES 6

This is a fragrant sauce. We serve this devilishly hot "gravy" over linguine at **Claire's,** and our customers love it.

    ½ cup olive oil
    8 large cloves garlic, minced
    1 small carrot, scrubbed and finely chopped
    1 teaspoon crushed red pepper flakes
    2 pounds mushrooms, larger ones sliced, smaller ones halved
    ¼ cup red wine
Two 28-ounce cans Italian whole peeled tomatoes, crushed with your hands
    ¼ cup chopped flat-leaf parsley
    1 teaspoon dried thyme
    1 teaspoon fennel seeds
    ¼ cup chopped fresh basil
    1 pound firm tofu, cut into ½-inch cubes (optional)
      Salt and black pepper to taste
    1 pound linguine

Heat the oil in a heavy pot over low heat. Add the garlic, carrot, red pepper flakes, and mushrooms. Cook about 10 minutes, stirring frequently, until the mushrooms are softened. Add the wine, raise the heat to medium, and cook for 3 minutes, stirring frequently. Add the tomatoes, parsley, thyme, fennel seeds, tofu if desired, salt, and pepper. Bring to a low boil and simmer about 30 minutes, stirring frequently, until the mushrooms are tender. Taste for seasoning.

Cook the linguine according to the package directions. Drain and turn into a serving bowl. Spoon ¼ of the sauce over the top and toss well. Spoon the remaining sauce over the top.

Tomato-Cream Sauce

SERVES 6

This rich sauce is irresistible. You know you've gone past the "tasting" limit when there isn't enough sauce for the pasta. Do try to save enough to toss over potato gnocchi. You can find gnocchi in the frozen pasta section of most supermarkets.

    4 tablespoons (½ stick) butter, cut into pieces
    4 shallots, chopped
    1 bunch scallions, white plus 3 inches green, sliced into ¼-inch pieces
    6 large, ripe tomatoes, chopped
    2 teaspoons dried dill weed
      Salt and black pepper to taste
      Broccoli florets from 1 bunch broccoli, chopped
    2 cups heavy cream
    2 cups whole milk
    ½ cup grated Parmesan
    2 pounds frozen potato gnocchi

Melt the butter in a large skillet over low heat. Add the shallots and scallions. Cook for 5 minutes, stirring frequently, until the scallions soften. Add the tomatoes, dill weed, salt, and pepper. Raise the heat to medium, cover, and cook 30 minutes, stirring frequently, until the tomatoes are soft. Lower the heat if the tomatoes begin to stick.

Meanwhile, steam the broccoli florets until tender. Set aside.

When the tomatoes are soft, add the cream and milk. Bring to a low boil, uncovered, and simmer about 10 minutes, stirring frequently, until the mixture is slightly reduced. (When you add the gnocchi to the sauce later it will thicken more.) Stir in the Parmesan and broccoli florets; keep the sauce warm.

Cook the gnocchi according to the package directions. Drain. Add the gnocchi to the sauce. Raise the heat to medium and cook, stirring constantly, for 2 minutes, until the sauce has coated the gnocchi.

Creamy Basil Sauce

SERVES 6

While we try to serve low-cholesterol sauces at **Claire's,** we sometimes splurge on an occasional cream sauce. We serve this with potato gnocchi or cheese tortellini.

> 4 tablespoons (½ stick) butter, cut into pieces
> 4 shallots, chopped
> 1 cup chopped fresh basil
> 3 tablespoons flour
> 2 cups heavy cream
> 2 cups milk
> Salt and black pepper to taste
> 2 pounds frozen gnocchi or cheese tortellini (found in the frozen pasta
>   section of your supermarket)

Melt the butter in a large skillet over low heat. Add the shallots and cook for 5 minutes, stirring frequently, until soft. Stir in the basil. Whisk in the flour and continue whisking until smooth. The mixture should bubble gently. Cook, whisking frequently, for 5 minutes; do not allow to brown. Gradually add the cream and milk, stirring well. Add the salt and pepper. Raise the heat to medium-low, and bring to a simmer. Continue cooking, stirring frequently, about 20 minutes, until the sauce coats the back of a spoon; keep it warm.

Cook the pasta according to the package directions. Drain. Add to the cream sauce. Raise the heat to medium. Cook, stirring constantly, for 2 minutes, until well mixed.

Spinach, Olive Oil, and Garlic Sauce

SERVES 6

This simple and delicious combination is perfect for any pasta. I especially like it over brown rice or potato gnocchi.

¼ cup olive oil
6 large cloves garlic, chopped
One 1-pound bag fresh spinach, chopped
¼ teaspoon crushed red pepper flakes
Salt and black pepper to taste
2 pounds frozen potato gnocchi (found in the frozen pasta section of your supermarket)

Heat the oil in a skillet over low heat. Add the garlic and cook for 3 minutes, until the garlic is softened. Add the spinach, red pepper flakes, salt, and pepper. Raise the heat slightly, cover, and cook about 15 minutes, stirring occasionally, until tender; keep the sauce warm.

Cook the gnocchi according to the package directions. Drain and add to the spinach sauce. Stir to combine well. Heat through and serve.

Hunter's Sauce

SERVES 6

This is every bit as good as the classic Italian sausage and pepper sauces I enjoyed in grinder sandwiches at carnivals during my teens. At **Claire's,** we serve this richly flavored sauce over pasta to grateful customers, who are happy to have a cholesterol-free, absolutely delicious "sausage." We use Light Life tofu Italian sausage links. You can find them in the frozen food section of most health-food stores.

    ½ cup olive oil
One 10-ounce package frozen tofu sausage, each link cut into 4 pieces (cut
       links while partly frozen)
    6 large cloves garlic, chopped
    3 bell peppers, 1 each yellow, red, and green, seeded and chopped
    1 medium red onion, chopped
    1 pound mushrooms, sliced
    ½ teaspoon fennel seeds
    ¼ teaspoon crushed red pepper flakes
    ½ teaspoon dried rosemary
    Salt and black pepper to taste
Two 28-ounce cans Italian whole peeled tomatoes, crushed with your hands
    1 pound rigatoni or other pasta

Heat 2 tablespoons of the olive oil in a nonstick skillet over medium heat. Add the sausage and brown all sides evenly. Set aside. In a heavy pot, heat the remaining ¼ cup plus 2 tablespoons olive oil over low heat. Add the garlic and cook 2 minutes, stirring frequently, until softened. Add the peppers, onion, mushrooms, fennel seeds, red pepper flakes, rosemary, salt, and pepper. Cover, raise the heat to medium-low, and cook for 15 minutes, stirring frequently, until the peppers are softened. Add the tomatoes, bring to a low boil, and simmer for 30 minutes, stirring frequently. Taste for seasoning. Keep the sauce warm.

Cook the pasta according to the package directions. Drain and turn into a serving bowl. Spoon ¼ of the sauce over the top and toss to coat the pasta. Spoon the remaining sauce over the top. Grind additional black pepper over the top if desired.

Cabbage-Mushroom Sauce

SERVES 6

This combination is splendid tossed over spinach-and-egg fettuccine.

½ cup olive oil
6 cloves garlic, chopped
1 medium red onion, diced
1 medium savoy cabbage, chopped
½ cup chopped flat-leaf parsley
1 pound mushrooms, sliced
1 tablespoon dried dill weed
Salt and black pepper to taste
¼ cup water
1 pound spinach-and-egg fettuccine

Heat the oil in a large pot over medium-low heat. Add the garlic and onion. Cook for 10 minutes, stirring often, until softened but not brown. Add the cabbage, parsley, mushrooms, dill weed, salt, pepper, and water. Cover, raise the heat to medium, and cook for 30 minutes, stirring frequently, until the cabbage is soft. Taste for seasoning. Keep the sauce warm.

Cook the fettuccine according to the package directions. Drain and turn into a serving bowl. Spoon ¼ of the cabbage mixture over the top and toss well. Spoon the remaining sauce over the top. Grind additional black pepper over the top if desired.

Alfredo Sauce

SERVES 6

This recipe was given to me by my neighbor Nancy Valentino. She is a great cook and a wise woman. The recipe came with a gentle warning: "This sauce is fantastic but too rich." She is right on both counts, so we do make this at **Claire's,** but not very often.

    4 tablespoons (½ stick) butter, cut into pieces
    2 cups heavy cream
    2 cups milk
    4 ounces shredded mozzarella
    1 pound ricotta
      Pinch nutmeg
  ¼ cup grated Parmesan
    1 bunch broccoli, bottom 1 inch of stems removed and discarded, chopped
       and steamed until crisp-tender (optional)
      Salt and black pepper to taste
    1 pound spinach fettuccine

Melt the butter in a large skillet over low heat. Stir in the cream and milk. Cook, stirring frequently, until warm. Add the mozzarella and stir until the cheese melts. Add the ricotta, nutmeg, and Parmesan. Cook, stirring constantly, until heated through. Add the broccoli if using, salt, and pepper. Stir to mix well. Taste for seasoning.

Keep the cream sauce warm while cooking the fettuccine according to the package directions. Drain and return the pasta to the pot it was cooked in. Pour the Alfredo Sauce over the top and toss well. Turn into a serving bowl.

Baked Pasta
with Florentine Sauce

SERVES 6

This dish is my frequent choice when I invite a large group for dinner. It's popular with all ages.

 ¼ cup olive oil
 4 large cloves garlic, minced
 1 medium red onion, finely chopped
 1 pound mushrooms, sliced
One 10-ounce bag fresh spinach, chopped
 4 medium tomatoes, chopped
 8 fresh basil leaves, chopped
   Salt and black pepper to taste
 1 pound low-fat ricotta
 4 ounces shredded low-fat mozzarella
 ¼ cup grated Parmesan
 1 pound penne
 ¼ cup bread crumbs

Heat the olive oil in a skillet over low heat. Add the garlic and onion and cook for 10 minutes, stirring frequently, until the onions are soft. Add the mushrooms, spinach, tomatoes, and basil. Sprinkle with salt and pepper. Raise the heat to medium-low, cover, and cook, stirring frequently, until the mushrooms are tender, about 20 minutes. Remove from the heat. Stir in the ricotta, mozzarella, and Parmesan. Mix until well combined. Set aside.

Preheat the oven to 350 degrees. Cook the pasta according to the package directions. Drain and turn into a large bowl. Spoon the sauce over the top and toss well. Turn into a rectangular glass baking dish. Sprinkle with the bread crumbs. Bake for 20 minutes, until heated through.

Creamy Shallot and Tarragon Sauce

SERVES 6

This is my interpretation of the memorable sauce I once enjoyed on a chicken dish at a lovely French restaurant in south Florida.

4 tablespoons (½ stick) butter, cut into 4 pieces
6 shallots, chopped
1 teaspoon dried tarragon or 1 tablespoon fresh tarragon, chopped
3 tablespoons flour
¼ cup white wine
4 cups half-and-half
   Salt and black pepper to taste
3 medium carrots, peeled, cut into matchsticks and steamed until just tender
1 bunch broccoli, florets only, chopped and steamed until just tender
1 pound egg noodles

Melt the butter in a large skillet over low heat. Add the shallots and cook for 5 minutes, stirring frequently, until soft. Stir in the tarragon. Whisk in the flour and continue whisking until smooth. The mixture should bubble gently. Cook, whisking frequently, for 5 minutes; do not allow to brown. Whisk in the wine. Bring to a low boil and simmer, whisking frequently, for 3 minutes. Gradually add the half-and-half, whisking until smooth. Add the salt and pepper. Simmer about 20 minutes, whisking frequently, until slightly thickened. Stir in the steamed carrots and broccoli. Taste for seasoning.

Keep the sauce warm while cooking the noodles according to the package directions. Drain the noodles and turn into the skillet of sauce. Toss well. Cook over low heat, stirring constantly, until heated through and combined.

My Mom's Cauliflower Sauce

SERVES 6

We serve this light, cholesterol-free sauce over angel-hair pasta at **Claire's.** Its delicate flavor is popular with everyone from toddlers to very senior adults.

> ½ cup olive oil
> 4 large cloves garlic, chopped
> 2 small heads cauliflower, cored and finely chopped
> 1 cup chopped flat-leaf parsley
> Two 28-ounce cans Italian whole peeled tomatoes, crushed with your hands
> ½ cup water
> Salt and black pepper to taste
> 1 pound angel-hair pasta
> Grated Parmesan or Romano (optional)

Heat the oil in a large pot over low heat. Add the garlic and cook for 1 minute, stirring frequently. Add the cauliflower and parsley. Cover and cook for 15 minutes, stirring frequently, until the cauliflower is softened. Add the tomatoes, water, salt, and pepper. Cover and simmer for 30 minutes, stirring frequently. Remove the cover and simmer for 20 to 30 minutes, stirring frequently, until the cauliflower is tender and the sauce is cooked. Taste for seasoning.

Keep the sauce warm while cooking the pasta according to the package directions. Drain and turn into a serving bowl. Spoon ¼ of the sauce over the pasta and toss well. Spoon the remaining sauce over the pasta. Grind additional black pepper over the top if desired. Serve with freshly grated Parmesan or Romano if desired.

Corner Copia Sauce

SERVES 6

This chunky sauce is perfect with any pasta, and is excellent spooned over thick slices of Italian bread, which is how we taste it for seasoning. You might want to double this recipe, or there might not be enough for the pasta after everyone helps to taste.

 ½ cup olive oil
 8 large cloves garlic, chopped
 1 medium yellow onion, chopped
 ¼ cup chopped flat-leaf parsley
One 10-ounce box frozen sliced artichoke hearts
 ¼ cup sliced black olives
Two 28-ounce cans Italian whole peeled tomatoes, crushed with your hands
 1 teaspoons dried basil or ¼ cup chopped fresh basil
 1 teaspoon dried oregano
 ½ teaspoon crushed red pepper flakes
 1 bay leaf
  Salt to taste
 1 teaspoon black pepper
 1 pound rigatoni or other pasta

Heat the oil in a large pot over low heat. Add the garlic and onion and cook for 5 minutes, stirring frequently, until soft. Add the parsley, artichoke hearts, and olives. Cook for 5 minutes, stirring frequently. Add the tomatoes, basil, oregano, red pepper flakes, bay leaf, salt, and pepper. Raise the heat to medium-low and simmer, stirring frequently, for 35 to 40 minutes, until the sauce is slightly reduced and tastes cooked. Taste for seasoning.

Keep the sauce warm while cooking the pasta according to the package directions. Drain and turn into a serving bowl. Spoon a little sauce over the top and toss well. Spoon the remaining sauce over the top.

Escarole and Beans for Pasta

SERVES 6

This thicker version of our Escarole and Bean Soup goes over ziti or penne. It's a favorite at **Claire's.** Be sure to serve plenty of crusty Italian bread for dunking.

    1 pound great northern beans, picked over
    3 quarts water
    8 cloves garlic, chopped
    ½ cup olive oil
    ½ teaspoon crushed red pepper flakes
    2 large heads escarole, chopped
      Salt and black pepper to taste
    1 pound ziti or penne

Put the beans and water in a large pot. Cover and bring to a boil over high heat. Lower the heat to medium and simmer uncovered for 1 hour, stirring frequently. Add the garlic, olive oil, and red pepper flakes. Continue simmering for 1 to 1½ hours, stirring frequently, until the beans are just tender. Add the escarole, salt, and pepper, and continue simmering for 30 minutes, stirring frequently, until the escarole is tender and the beans are soft. Taste for seasoning.

Keep the sauce warm while cooking the pasta according to the package directions. Drain the pasta, add to the escarole and beans, and toss well. Turn into a serving bowl. Grind additional black pepper over the top if desired.

Broccoli Rabe for Linguine

SERVES 6

Broccoli rabe, or bitter broccoli, can be found throughout the year in the produce section of your supermarket or at your Italian market. Take advantage of this delicious, vitamin-packed vegetable. Serve this sauce with Italian bread for dunking.

> ½ cup olive oil
> 6 large cloves garlic, chopped
> ½ to 1 teaspoon crushed red pepper flakes
> 1 tablespoon fennel seeds
> 3 bunches broccoli rabe (about 3 pounds), washed and chopped into 4-inch
> pieces
> ¾ cup water
> Salt and black pepper to taste
> 1 pound linguine

Heat the oil in a large pot over low heat. Add the garlic and cook for 2 minutes, stirring frequently; do not allow to brown. Add the red pepper flakes, fennel seeds, and broccoli rabe. Stir to coat with the oil. Add the water, salt, and pepper. Cover and raise the heat to medium-low. Simmer about 40 minutes, stirring frequently, until the broccoli rabe is tender. Taste for seasoning.

Keep the sauce warm while cooking the pasta according to the package directions. Drain and turn the pasta into the pot of cooked broccoli rabe. Toss well and turn into a serving bowl.

Acorn Squash Sauce

SERVES 8

My mom uses butternut squash for her version of this sauce, but we use acorn squash at **Claire's.** It's just as tasty and much easier to cut before cooking, making it more practical for our busy restaurant.

    4 large acorn squash, cut in half and seeded
    ½ cup olive oil
    6 large cloves garlic, chopped
    1 bunch flat-leaf parsley, chopped
    ¼ cup chopped fresh basil leaves
      Salt and black pepper to taste
    1 pound linguine

Preheat the oven to 425 degrees. Arrange the acorn squash, cut side down, in a single layer in a baking pan. Using a fork, pierce each shell in 4 places. Pour water into the pan to ½ inch. Cover the pan with foil. Bake about 1 hour, or until the squash is very soft when pierced with a fork. When the squash is cool enough to handle, use a spoon to scoop the pulp into a bowl. Set aside.

Heat the oil in a large skillet over medium-low heat. Add the garlic, parsley, and basil. Cook, stirring frequently, for 10 minutes, until the garlic is softened and golden, but not dark brown. Add the squash, salt, and pepper and cook for 25 to 30 minutes, stirring frequently, until heated through and well mixed. Taste for seasoning.

Keep the sauce warm while you cook the linguine according to the package directions. Drain and turn into a serving bowl. Spoon some sauce over the top and toss well. Spoon the remaining sauce over the top. Serve with additional freshly ground black pepper if desired.

Butternut, Acorn, and Pumpkin Squash Sauce

SERVES 8

This combination of tastes and textures is exceptional. Butternut and acorn squash are generally found year-round, but pumpkin squash (calabazo) is usually available only during fall and winter. Pumpkin squash grows in a huge, elongated pumpkin shape and has dark orange pulp, which makes a flavorful sauce. Most supermarkets cut this giant squash into 1- or 2-pound pieces.

2 large acorn squash, cut in half and seeded
1 large butternut squash, peeled, cut in half lengthwise, and seeded
2 to 4 pounds pumpkin squash (calabazo), peeled
½ cup olive oil
8 large cloves garlic, chopped
½ cup chopped flat-leaf parsley
¼ cup chopped fresh basil
¼ cup water
   Salt and black pepper to taste
1 pound linguine

Preheat the oven to 425 degrees. Arrange the acorn squash halves in a single layer, cut side down, in a baking pan. Using a fork, pierce the shells in 4 places. Pour water into the pan to ½ inch. Cover the pan with foil. Bake about 1 hour, or until the squash is tender when pierced with a fork.

Meanwhile, cut the butternut and pumpkin squash into 1-inch cubes and set aside. When the acorn squash is tender, remove from the oven and set aside to cool for handling.

Heat the oil in a large skillet over medium-low heat. Add the garlic, butternut and pumpkin squash, parsley, and basil. Stir to coat the squash cubes. Add the water, salt, and pepper. Cover and cook, stirring occasionally, about 1 hour, until tender.

Scoop out the cooled pulp from the acorn squash and add to the skillet, stirring well. Taste for seasoning.

Keep the sauce warm while you cook the linguine according to the package directions. Drain and turn into a serving bowl. Spoon some sauce over the top and toss well. Spoon the remaining sauce over the top. Grind additional black pepper over the top if desired.

Mushrooms Stroganoff

SERVES 8

We serve this rich sauce over spinach fettuccine and our customers love it. While we prefer to serve nondairy tomato sauces, we give in to this temptation often.

- 8 tablespoons (1 stick) butter, cut into pieces
- 2 large cloves garlic, minced
- ½ large yellow onion, chopped
- 1 pound mushrooms, sliced into ¼-inch pieces
- 2 tablespoons flour
- 2 cups low-fat sour cream
- ½ tablespoon dried dill weed
- 2 tablespoons dry sherry or Marsala
- Salt and black pepper to taste
- 1 pound spinach fettuccine

Melt the butter in a large skillet over low heat. Add the garlic and onion and cook for 5 minutes, stirring frequently. Add the mushrooms, raise the heat to medium, and continue cooking for 20 minutes, stirring occasionally, until the mushrooms are soft. Sprinkle the flour evenly over the top and stir well. Cook for 10 minutes, stirring frequently. Stir in the sour cream, dill weed, sherry or Marsala, salt, and pepper. Cook, stirring constantly, until heated through and thickened, about 10 minutes. Taste for seasoning.

Keep the sauce warm while you cook the fettuccine according to the package directions. Drain and turn into the skillet of sauce. Toss well.

Bean Sauce for Rice or Pasta

SERVES 8

This is a popular Italian dish, and you can find it once a week at my mother's, at my mother-in-law's, and at **Claire's.** My father-in-law always dunks bread spread with peanut butter in his rice or pasta with bean sauce, and weird as it may sound, it's fantastic. Try it.

　　　1 pound red kidney beans, picked over
　　　3 quarts water
　　　½ cup olive oil
　　　6 large cloves garlic, chopped
　　　½ cup chopped flat-leaf parsley
　One 6-ounce can tomato paste
　　　　Salt and black pepper to taste
　　　1 pound brown rice or pasta elbows, cooked

Place the beans and water in a large covered pot over high heat. Bring to a boil, remove the cover, and lower the heat to medium. Add the olive oil. Simmer uncovered, stirring frequently, for 1½ hours, until the beans are barely tender. Add the garlic, parsley, and tomato paste. Continue simmering, stirring frequently, for another 45 minutes to 1 hour, until the beans are tender. Add salt and pepper. Spoon the sauce over cooked rice or pasta. Sprinkle with additional freshly ground black pepper.

Arrabiata Sauce

SERVES 8

This is my interpretation of a spicy sauce I enjoyed at Genarro's in New Haven, one of my favorite restaurants. Our customers love this sauce over rigatoni.

½ cup extra-virgin olive oil
8 large cloves garlic, quartered
3 large yellow onions, thickly sliced
4 hot cherry peppers, chopped (wash your hands after chopping)
  Pinch crushed red pepper flakes
1 pound mushrooms, sliced
½ cup chopped flat-leaf parsley
1 teaspoon dried rosemary or 1 tablespoon chopped fresh rosemary
½ cup white wine
Two 28-ounce cans Italian whole peeled tomatoes, crushed with your hands
  Salt and black pepper to taste
1 pound rigatoni

Heat the oil in a large skillet over low heat. Add the garlic and onions, cover, and cook for 20 minutes, stirring frequently, until soft. Add the cherry peppers, red pepper flakes, mushrooms, parsley, and rosemary. Continue cooking, covered, for 15 minutes, stirring frequently, until the mushrooms are softened. Stir in the wine and tomatoes and sprinkle with salt and pepper. Raise the heat to medium and bring to a low boil, uncovered. Simmer uncovered for 40 minutes, stirring frequently, until the sauce is slightly thickened. Taste for seasoning.

Keep the sauce warm while you cook the pasta according to the package directions. Drain and turn into a serving bowl. Spoon some sauce over the top and toss well. Spoon the remaining sauce over the top.

Summer Pesto

MAKES ABOUT 1 PINT

Fresh basil is our favorite herb at **Claire's,** and during the summer months, when it grows in abundance, we use it by the crate. We celebrate basil season by making pesto every day. We add a little to our minestrone, mix some into the ricotta filling for our lasagna and eggplant rollatini, and toss it with our pasta and potato salads.

    1½ cups olive oil
      4 large cloves garlic, chopped
      2 large bunches basil, leaves and thin stems chopped
      3 tablespoons chopped walnuts
    ¼ cup chopped parsley
      2 tablespoons grated Parmesan
      1 teaspoon black pepper
        Salt to taste

Put all the ingredients in the work bowl of a food processor fitted with the metal blade. Process on high speed for 30 seconds, stopping 2 or 3 times to scrape down the sides with a rubber spatula. Taste for seasoning.

Winter Pesto

MAKES ABOUT 1 PINT

My husband, Frank, is a good cook, and will sometimes make something wonderful for our customers at **Claire's.** This is his winter pesto, which we enjoy when fresh basil is not available. It keeps us happy until our farm markets get their beautiful bunches of the fresh herb.

    1¼ cups olive oil
     5 large cloves garlic, chopped
     4 cups packed fresh spinach, cleaned and chopped
     1 tablespoon dried basil
     3 tablespoons chopped walnuts
     3 tablespoons grated Parmesan
    ½ teaspoon black pepper
       Salt to taste

Measure the olive oil into the work bowl of a food processor fitted with the metal blade. Add the remaining ingredients. Process on high speed for 30 seconds, stopping 2 or 3 times to scrape down the sides with a rubber spatula. Taste for seasoning.

Mexican Dishes

We have been preparing Mexican foods at **Claire's** since the late seventies, and our sales of them have soared along with what seems to be a national trend. Mexican-style cooking provides an exciting and flavorful way to eat your vegetables, beans, and grains. These simple and basic meals made with good-quality ingredients appeal to many people, young and old. Our Mexican dishes at **Claire's** have always been prepared mild to medium-hot. If you haven't already developed a taste for hot and spicy foods, I suggest you start out using small amounts of spices and peppers when following our recipes and increase the fire as you wish. One of the many attractions of Mexican food is that it tastes a bit exotic, but the ingredients can usually be found at the supermarket. And flour and corn tortillas can be stored in your freezer for added convenience.

Guacamole

SERVES 8

This recipe for guacamole is delicious and simple to make. Just remember the basics: start with perfectly ripened avocados, and prepare the guacamole just before you plan to serve it. Once an avocado is cut open, it will not continue to ripen and cannot be saved. Test an avocado for ripeness by gently pressing its skin in several places. If it feels uniformly soft, the avocado is ready to be cut open and enjoyed. Guacamole makes a great dip for corn chips, and we love it in a pita bread sandwich, topped with lettuce, tomatoes, and sprouts. We use at least a case of avocados a day at **Claire's,** mostly by spooning dollops of guacamole onto enchiladas, veggie burgers, tuna salad sandwiches, and most of our Mexican casseroles. Surprise your family with chips and guacamole before dinner.

> 5 ripe avocados, peeled and pitted
> ½ small yellow onion, chopped
> 2 tablespoons olive oil
> Juice of 1 lemon
> Salt and black pepper to taste

Place the avocado pulp with the remaining ingredients in a bowl. Mash together, using a potato masher, until soft but still chunky. Taste for seasoning. Serve immediately.

Salsa

MAKES ABOUT 1 QUART

Our customers like our Salsa so much that we sell it for take-home. At the restaurant, we serve it with our chips and on our enchiladas, burritos, Eggplant Veracruz (see page 180), and other Mexican dishes. It's delicious in the dressing we use for our Mexican Pasta Salad too (see page 99). Make a double batch for the weekend.

    ¼ cup olive oil
    2 small onions, chopped
    6 cloves garlic, minced
    2 teaspoons chili powder
    ¼ teaspoon crushed red pepper flakes, or more to taste
One 4-ounce can peeled green chili peppers, chopped
One 28-ounce can whole tomatoes in juice
    ½ cup chopped cilantro or parsley
       Salt and black pepper to taste

Heat the oil in a large pot over low heat. Add the onions, garlic, chili powder, red pepper flakes, and chili peppers. Cook uncovered over low heat for 15 minutes, stirring occasionally, until the onions are soft. Add the tomatoes, cilantro or parsley, salt, and pepper. Simmer for 30 minutes, stirring frequently. Taste for seasoning.

Napolito Pancakes

SERVES 4

Benne Gutierrez, one of our many talented cooks, is from Mexico. He used to bring in new foods for us to try at **Claire's**, exotic peppers, cornhusks for tamales, and *napolitos* (cactus). Although I've never been able to locate fresh cactus for our restaurant, canned *napolitos* are available in many supermarkets. *Napolitos* taste like steamed green bell peppers, are very good in a Mexican frittata, and make delicious fritter-like pancakes. We serve them with Salsa (see page 164), Benne's Special Sauce (see page 166), or low-fat sour cream, and they are wonderful either hot or chilled, which makes them great picnic food.

    1 cup flour
    1 teaspoon baking powder
    ½ teaspoon salt
       Black pepper to taste
    ½ teaspoon chili powder
    2 tablespoons chopped cilantro
    2 eggs
    ½ cup milk
    1 teaspoon olive oil
One 8-ounce can *napolitos,* chopped
    ¼ cup soybean or vegetable oil for frying

Into a mixing bowl, sift the flour, baking powder, salt, pepper, and chili powder. In a separate bowl, beat together the cilantro, eggs, milk, and olive oil until well blended. Pour the liquid mixture over the dry mixture all at once and, using a spoon, mix lightly to combine. Stir in the *napolitos.*

Heat the oil in a nonstick skillet or griddle over medium-low heat. The oil is ready when a pinch of flour rises quickly to the top. Drop the batter by heaping tablespoons into the hot oil. Cook on each side about 2 minutes, until golden brown. Do not cook the pancakes too quickly or the centers will be raw. Drain on a double thickness of paper towels while you fry the remaining batter.

Benne's Special Sauce

MAKES ABOUT 1½ CUPS

The first time Benne made this marvelous sauce from his homeland, Mexico, we lost control during the sampling. Before we knew it, we had "tasted" a quart and had to quickly prepare more for our customers. We served it as a dip for corn chips, as a sauce with our Napolito Pancakes (see page 165), and baked with enchiladas, and we are often tempted to eat it by the spoonful.

    2 fresh jalapeño peppers
    4 fresh tomatillos or green tomatoes
    2 ripe avocados, peeled and pitted
    ½ small yellow onion, chopped
    1 cup chopped flat-leaf parsley
    ¼ cup chopped cilantro
    4 large cloves garlic, chopped
      Juice of 1 lemon
      Juice of 1 lime
    1 cup low-fat sour cream
      Salt and black pepper to taste

Place the jalapeño peppers and tomatillos or green tomatoes in a small saucepan. Cover with water and bring to a boil over high heat. Cook for 10 minutes, stirring occasionally. Remove from the heat, drain, and cool slightly. In a blender place the cooked jalapeños and tomatillos, avocado pulp, onion, parsley, cilantro, garlic, and lemon and lime juice. Cover and blend on low speed for 20 seconds until pureed, stopping to scrape down the sides as needed. Turn into a bowl. Stir in the sour cream, salt, and pepper. Taste for seasoning.

Mexican Rice

SERVES 6

For a perfect meal, serve this colorful dish with melted Monterey Jack cheese on top, along with a green salad tossed with some black beans and a hot pepper-spiked vinaigrette.

    ¼ cup olive oil
    1 small red onion, chopped
    3 bell peppers, 1 each red, yellow, and green, seeded and chopped
    1 carrot, finely chopped
    1 small yellow onion, chopped
      Corn kernels cut from 3 ears, or one 10-ounce box frozen kernels
One 10-ounce box frozen green peas
    1 teaspoon chili powder
    3 tablespoons chopped cilantro or flat-leaf parsley
   10 cups cooked brown rice
      Salt and black pepper to taste
      Low-fat sour cream (optional)

Heat the oil in a large skillet over medium-low heat. Add the red onion, peppers, carrot, yellow onion, corn, peas, and chili powder. Cook for 15 minutes, stirring frequently, until the vegetables are crisp-tender. Stir in the cilantro or parsley, brown rice, salt, and pepper. Mix well and cook over medium-low heat an additonal 5 minutes, or till heated through. Taste for seasoning. Turn into a serving dish. Serve with low-fat sour cream if desired.

Refried Beans

SERVES 4 AS AN ENTREE

We have used this recipe for many years at **Claire's**. It's a great dip for corn chips and a delicious burrito filling, and makes a fiber-rich side dish. Serve it plain for a cholesterol-free meal or bake it with shredded low-fat Monterey Jack cheese or cheddar.

> **1 pound pinto beans, picked over**
> **¼ cup olive oil**
> **1 large onion, minced**
>   **Salt and black pepper to taste**

Cook the beans according to the package directions. Drain, reserving ¼ cup of the cooking liquid. Heat the oil in a large skillet over low heat. Add the onion, cover, and cook for 15 minutes, stirring frequently, until soft. Add the drained pinto beans, reserved cooking liquid, salt, and pepper. Fry the beans in the skillet about 10 minutes, stirring frequently. Mash the beans in the skillet with a potato masher until creamy and smooth. Taste for seasoning.

Soft Bean and Cheese Tacos

SERVES 4

We began making meatless Mexican food at **Claire's** back in the late seventies, and our customers responded with such enthusiasm that we wanted to do more. Our crisp corn tacos, the kind that crumble apart as you eat them, have been replaced by these easy-to-enjoy soft tacos, made with flour tortillas. They're great for lunch or dinner, or as part of a Mexican buffet.

Eight 6-inch flour tortillas
    2 cups Refried Beans, heated (see page 168)
    8 ounces shredded Monterey Jack cheese
    2 cups finely chopped romaine
    1 large tomato, finely chopped
    ½ small yellow onion, minced
    1 cup Salsa, heated (see page 164)
        Low-fat sour cream (optional)

Hold a tortilla in one hand and fill it using your other hand. Spread about ¼ cup heated Refried Beans along the bottom of the tortilla. Sprinkle a little shredded Monterey Jack over the beans. Arrange about ¼ cup of chopped romaine over the cheese, then scatter some chopped tomato and onion across the top. Spoon 2 tablespoons heated Salsa evenly over the top. Stand the taco in a taco holder or in a bowl while you repeat the process with the remaining tortillas. Serve with low-fat sour cream if desired.

Enchiladas

SERVES 6

These enchiladas first appeared at **Claire's** as a special of the day. We sold out every time we offered them, so we added them to our permanent menu. They remain popular today at lunch or dinner.

4 tablespoons (½ stick) butter, cut into 4 pieces
1 small onion, chopped
2 cloves garlic, minced
1 pound mushrooms, sliced into ¼-inch pieces
Corn kernels cut from 3 ears, or one 10-ounce box frozen kernels
Two 10-ounce bags fresh spinach, washed and chopped
1 teaspoon chili powder
12 ounces shredded Monterey Jack cheese
2 cups low-fat sour cream
Black pepper to taste
Twelve 6-inch corn tortillas
Soybean or vegetable oil for brushing the tortillas
2 cups Salsa (see page 164)
Avocado slices (optional)

Preheat the oven to 400 degrees. Melt the butter in a large skillet over medium-low heat. Add the onion, garlic, mushrooms, and corn. Cook about 15 minutes, stirring occasionally, until the onions are softened. Add the spinach and chili powder. Cover and cook for 20 minutes, stirring occasionally, until the spinach is wilted. Stir in ½ the cheese. Mix well until melted. Add the sour cream and pepper and mix well. Remove from the heat and cool slightly.

Brush both sides of each tortilla with a little oil. Spoon just less than ⅓ cup of the filling into the center of each tortilla. Roll one side of the tortilla over the filling, then roll the other side over. Place the filled tortilla, seam side down, in a rectangular glass baking dish. Repeat with the remaining tortillas, placing them in the baking dish in a single layer. Spoon the Salsa over the enchiladas and sprinkle with the remaining cheese.

Bake for 15 minutes, or until the Salsa is hot and bubbly and the cheese is melted. Serve with slices of ripe avocado if desired.

Challapitas

SERVES 6

These make a great dinner when teamed up with Mexican rice and a tossed salad. You can fry the tortillas up to three days in advance and store them, unrefrigerated, in a covered container.

  Six 6-inch corn tortillas
    2 to 4 tablespoons soybean or vegetable oil for frying the tortillas
    2 cups Refried Beans, heated (see page 168)
    1 recipe Guacamole (see page 163)
1½ cups low-fat sour cream
    1 large tomato, diced
    3 tablespoons chopped cilantro

Brush the sides of each tortilla with oil. Heat a nonstick skillet over medium heat. Fry each side of each tortilla until crisp, about 30 seconds. Set aside until cool enough to handle. Layer each tortilla in the following order: ⅓ cup Refried Beans, ⅙ of the Guacamole, and ¼ cup sour cream. Top each challapita with some diced tomato and cilantro. Serve immediately.

Quesadillas

SERVES 6

Quesadillas are popular with young and old at **Claire's**. We serve them with Salsa, Refried Beans, Guacamole, or low-fat sour cream, as an appetizer or with a bowl of soup or salad for dinner. We fry the flour tortillas up to 2 days in advance and store them, unrefrigerated, in a covered container. Once they are fried, they are fragile, so we stack them between paper towels for cushioning. If any do happen to break, don't despair; just sprinkle the pieces with confectioners' sugar and cinnamon and you'll have a delicious sweet snack.

    Six 10-inch flour tortillas
       4 or 5 tablespoons soybean or vegetable oil for frying
    12 ounces shredded Monterey Jack cheese
       Paprika for dusting
       2 cups Salsa (see page 164)

Preheat the oven to 400 degrees. Heat the oil in a large nonstick skillet over medium heat. Fry each side of each tortilla about 20 seconds, until golden brown and crisp. Drain on double layers of paper towels.

Arrange the fried tortillas in a single layer on cookie sheets. Sprinkle ¼ cup shredded Monterey Jack and a little paprika evenly over the top of each tortilla. Bake for 10 minutes, or until the cheese melts. Serve with Salsa for dipping.

Mexican Home Fries

SERVES 6

These potatoes are great hot or cold, for breakfast, lunch, or dinner.

9 large potatoes, cut into 1-inch cubes
¼ cup olive oil
4 cloves garlic, minced
Corn kernels cut from 3 ears, or one 10-ounce box frozen kernels
1 large onion, chopped
1 teaspoon chili powder
3 bell peppers, 1 each red, yellow, and green, chopped
1 large tomato, chopped
Salt and black pepper to taste
8 ounces shredded Monterey Jack cheese
Low-fat sour cream (optional)

Preheat the oven to 400 degrees. Boil the potatoes until barely tender, about 10 minutes. Reserving ¼ cup of the cooking liquid, drain the potatoes and set aside. Heat the oil in a large skillet over medium-low heat. Add the garlic, corn, onion, chili powder, and peppers. Cover and cook, stirring frequently, until the peppers are barely tender, about 5 minutes. Add the tomato, potatoes, reserved cooking liquid, salt, and pepper. Mix well. Cover and continue cooking until the peppers are tender, about 15 minutes.

Remove from the heat and turn into a baking dish. Sprinkle with the cheese. Bake about 15 minutes, until the cheese is melted. Serve with low-fat sour cream if desired.

Chili 1

SERVES 6

This chili is a wonderful food; it's a good balance of beans and grains, and a convenient meal made in a single pot and served in a bowl. With it, we offer melted cheddar, chopped red onion, sour cream, and corn chips. Chili can also be enjoyed in a burrito or taco. Like most bean dishes, it keeps well for up to 3 days, and actually improves in flavor.

    3 quarts water
    ½ pound red kidney beans, picked over
    ½ pound pinto beans, picked over
    1 medium yellow onion, chopped
    2 green bell peppers, seeded and chopped
    ¼ cup olive oil
    4 cloves garlic, chopped
    ½ cup chopped parsley
    1 teaspoon chili powder
One 28-ounce can whole peeled tomatoes, crushed with your hands
    Corn kernels cut from 3 ears, or one 10-ounce box frozen kernels
    2 cups cooked brown rice
    ½ teaspoon ground cumin
    Salt and black pepper to taste
    2 or 3 dashes Tabasco

Put the water and kidney beans in a large pot. Cover and bring to a boil over high heat. Lower the heat to medium-low and simmer uncovered for 45 minutes, stirring frequently. Add the pinto beans, onion, peppers, olive oil, garlic, parsley, chili powder, and tomatoes. Return to a boil and simmer about 1½ hours, stirring frequently, until the beans are tender. Add the corn and continue simmering for 15 minutes, stirring frequently. Stir in the cooked rice, cumin, salt, pepper, and Tabasco. Cook for 10 minutes, stirring frequently. Taste for seasoning.

Chili II

SERVES 8

This is my favorite chili, and the one I most often choose to cook at home. I like the combination of black beans with pinto beans and kidney beans, and the chunks of vegetables are so good. Enjoy this one-dish meal year-round.

    4 quarts water
    ½ pound red kidney beans, picked over
    ½ pound black beans, picked over
    ½ pound pinto beans, picked over
One 28-ounce can whole peeled tomatoes, crushed with your hands
    ¼ cup olive oil
    1 medium yellow onion, cut into 1-inch pieces
    3 carrots, chopped into ¾-inch chunks
    3 bell peppers, 1 each red, yellow, and green, cut into 1-inch pieces
    4 ribs celery, cut into ¾-inch chunks
    Corn kernels cut from 3 ears, or one 10-ounce box frozen kernels
    1 medium zucchini, cut into ½-inch pieces
    ¼ teaspoon crushed red pepper flakes, or to taste
    ¼ cup chopped cilantro or parsley
    1 tablespoon chili powder
    1 teaspoon ground cumin
    2 cups cooked brown rice
    Salt and black pepper to taste
    2 or 3 dashes Tabasco

Put the water and kidney beans into a large pot. Cover and bring to a boil over high heat. Lower the heat to medium-low and simmer uncovered for 45 minutes, stirring frequently. Add the black beans, pinto beans, tomatoes, and olive oil. Continue simmering, stirring frequently, for 1 hour. Add the onion, carrots, peppers, celery, corn, zucchini, red pepper flakes, cilantro or parsley, chili powder, and cumin. Continue simmering about 45 minutes, stirring frequently, until the beans and vegetables are tender. Stir in the cooked rice, salt, pepper, and Tabasco. Mix well and heat through. Taste for seasoning.

Santa Fe Chili

SERVES 6

One of our customers spent a year painting in New Mexico. She came back with beautiful work and an idea for a new dish. While she wasn't sure of the exact ingredients, she remembered enjoying a rich chili flavored with chocolate, and this recipe is our interpretation. The chocolate works nicely with the black beans.

1 pound black beans, picked over
3 quarts water
¼ cup olive oil
4 ounces unsweetened chocolate, broken into small pieces
2 cups brown rice, uncooked
2 cloves garlic, finely chopped
3 carrots, chopped into ¾-inch pieces
3 large, ripe tomatoes, seeded and cut into 1-inch pieces
2 green bell peppers, seeded and cut into 1-inch pieces
1 bunch scallions, white plus 3 inches green, cut into ½-inch lengths
2 tablespoons chili powder
¼ cup unsweetened cocoa powder
½ teaspoon crushed red pepper flakes
⅛ teaspoon ground cloves
    Corn kernels cut from 3 uncooked ears, or one 10-ounce box frozen
      kernels
    Salt and black pepper to taste
    Accompaniments to taste

Put the black beans and water in a large pot. Cover and bring to a boil over high heat. Reduce the heat to medium-low, uncover, and simmer for 1 hour, stirring frequently. Add the olive oil, chocolate, brown rice, garlic, carrots, tomatoes, peppers, scallions, chili powder, cocoa powder, red pepper flakes, and cloves. Continue simmering uncovered for 1½ hours, until the rice and beans are soft and the chili is stew-like in thickness. Stir in the corn kernels, salt, and pepper. Cook for 3 minutes, stirring frequently. Taste for seasoning. Serve with sour cream and chopped red onion if desired, and corn chips for dipping.

Tostadas

SERVES 4

These tostadas are popular with kids, who say they're fun to eat.

Six 6-inch corn tortillas
4 tablespoons soybean or vegetable oil for frying
2 cups Refried Beans, heated (see page 168)
1½ cups Salsa, heated (see page 164)
6 ounces shredded Monterey Jack cheese
3 cups finely chopped romaine
1 large tomato, diced
½ small yellow onion, chopped
½ cup low-fat sour cream
    Avocado slices (optional)

Preheat the oven to 400 degrees. Heat the oil in a nonstick skillet over medium heat. Fry the tortillas until just crisp on each side, about 30 seconds per side. Drain on a double layer of paper towels until cool enough to handle. Arrange the fried tortillas in a single layer on a cookie sheet lined with parchment paper. Spread each tortilla with ⅓ cup heated Refried Beans. Spoon ¼ cup heated Salsa over the beans. Sprinkle about 2 tablespoons shredded cheese evenly over the top of each tortilla.

Bake for 15 minutes, or until the cheese melts. Carefully transfer the tostadas to a large serving platter. Arrange chopped romaine over each tostada, then scatter diced tomatoes and chopped onions over each. Spoon a heaping tablespoon of sour cream into the center of each. Serve with sliced avocado if desired.

Vegetable Fajitas

SERVES 6

Fajitas are great and all the rage. As of this writing, we make them as a special, although I expect they will move to the permanent menu because of their considerable popularity. At home I like to serve them at a party. The guests can make their own fajitas and fill them with as much or as little as they want. Serve the fajitas with rice, a salad, and fresh fruit sangria.

¼ cup olive oil
1 small red onion, cut in half, then sliced thickly
1 small yellow onion, cut in half, then sliced thickly
2 cloves garlic, chopped
5 large bell peppers, a combination of yellow, red, and green, cut in half, seeded, and sliced into ½-inch ribs
3 large tomatoes, cut in half, then each half sliced into 5 wedges
1 teaspoon chili powder
¼ teaspoon crushed red pepper flakes, or to taste
   Juice of 1 lemon
   Juice of 1 lime
   Salt and black pepper to taste

Accompaniments:

Twelve 6-inch flour tortillas
     1 recipe Guacamole (see page 163)
     2 cups Refried Beans, heated (see page 168)
   1½ cups low-fat sour cream
   12 ounces shredded Monterey Jack cheese

Preheat the oven to 300 degrees. Heat the olive oil in a large skillet over medium heat. Add the onions and garlic. Cover and cook for 10 minutes, stirring frequently. Add the peppers, tomatoes, chili powder, and red pepper flakes. Cover and cook for 15 minutes, stirring frequently, until the peppers are crisp-

tender. Raise the heat to high, remove the cover, and add the lemon and lime juice, salt, and pepper. Continue cooking, stirring frequently, for 3 minutes, until the peppers are tender and lightly browned.

Keep the filling warm while you warm the tortillas for 3 minutes in the oven. Stack the warmed tortillas on a plate and cover with a cloth napkin. Turn the fajita filling onto a platter and arrange the accompaniments on a separate platter.

Eggplant Veracruz

SERVES 8

This is our Mexican version of the ever-popular eggplant parmigiana.

2 cups flour (or more) for dredging
6 eggs
3 tablespoons chopped flat-leaf parsley
   Salt and black pepper to taste
½ cup soybean or vegetable oil for frying
1 large eggplant, peeled and sliced lengthwise into ⅛-inch pieces
3 cups Salsa (see page 164)
8 ounces shredded Monterey Jack cheese

Preheat the oven to 375 degrees. Measure the flour into a shallow bowl and set aside. In a separate bowl, beat together the eggs, parsley, salt, and pepper. Set aside. Heat the oil in a large nonstick skillet over medium heat. Dredge the eggplant slices one at a time in the flour to coat both sides. Shake off the excess. Dip each slice into the beaten eggs. Lightly shake off the excess. Place the eggplant in the hot oil, filling the skillet without overlapping. Cook each side until golden brown, 1 minute or more. Drain the eggplant slices on a plate lined with a double thickness of paper towels. Repeat with remaining eggplant slices. If the oil begins to smoke or foam, heat fresh oil and fry the remaining eggplant slices.

Spread 1 cup Salsa in a rectangular glass baking dish. Stack the eggplant slices evenly in the dish. Pour the remaining Salsa on top. Sprinkle with the cheese. Bake for 30 minutes, until the Salsa is hot and the cheese is melted.

Eggplant and Tomato Burritos

SERVES 6

These burritos are a big hit at **Claire's** because they combine two favorites: Mexican food and eggplant. You can prepare the filling up to two days in advance and reheat it when you're ready to fill your tortillas.

    ¼ cup olive oil
    1 large eggplant, diced
    1 large onion, cut into ¼-inch rings
    4 large cloves garlic, minced
    3 tablespoons water
      Salt and black pepper to taste
    1 teaspoon chili powder
    2 large ripe tomatoes, chopped
    ¾ cup evaporated skimmed milk
 Six 10-inch flour tortillas
    4 to 6 ounces shredded Monterey Jack cheese
      Low-fat sour cream (optional)

Preheat the oven to 400 degrees. Heat the oil in a large, nonstick skillet over low heat. Add the eggplant, onion, and garlic. Cover and cook for 15 minutes, stirring frequently, until the eggplant softens. Add the water, salt, pepper, chili powder, and tomatoes. Raise the heat to medium, cover, and cook for 35 minutes, stirring frequently, until the eggplant is tender. Remove the cover, stir in the evaporated milk, and bring to a low boil. Simmer, stirring frequently, for 10 minutes, until the mixture thickens slightly.

To serve, arrange the flour tortillas on 2 cookie sheets that have either been covered with parchment paper or sprayed with nonstick cooking spray. Spoon one-sixth of the filling into the center of each tortilla. Roll each side of the tortilla over the filling and carefully turn each burrito so that the seam side is down. Sprinkle each with one-sixth of the shredded cheese. Bake for 15 minutes, until the cheese melts and the tortillas are golden brown. Serve with low-fat sour cream if desired.

Mixed-Vegetable Burritos

SERVES 4

We use this filling in flour tortillas, which we roll to the size of a huge manicotti rather than the smaller traditional burrito size, and this gives our customers substantially more of the savory filling. These burritos, served with a bean salad, make a satisfying meal.

    3 quarts water
    1 large potato, diced
    2 small zucchini, chopped
    2 small yellow squash, chopped
       Corn kernels cut from 3 ears, or one 10-ounce box frozen kernels
    3 bell peppers (red, green, yellow, or a combination), seeded and chopped
    1 large tomato, chopped
    1 small red onion, minced
    3 tablespoons chopped cilantro or flat-leaf parsley
    1 cup low-fat sour cream
    1 teaspoon chili powder
       Salt and black pepper to taste
  12 ounces shredded Monterey Jack cheese
Four 10-inch flour tortillas
       Avocado slices (optional)

Preheat the oven to 375 degrees. Bring the water to a boil in a covered pot over high heat. Add the potatoes, zucchini, yellow squash, corn, and peppers. Return to a boil and cook, uncovered, about 4 minutes, until the potatoes are just tender. Drain and turn into a bowl. Add the tomato, onion, cilantro or parsley, sour cream, chili powder, salt, pepper, and ½ the cheese. Toss gently. Taste for seasoning.

Arrange the tortillas in a single layer on cookie sheets lined with parchment paper. Spoon ¼ of the filling into the center of each tortilla. Fold the left side over the filling, then the right side over the left side, barely closing. Carefully turn the burritos seam side down. Sprinkle the burritos with the remaining cheese. Bake about 15 minutes, until the cheese is melted. Serve with additional sour cream and sliced avocado if desired.

Mexican Stuffed Peppers

SERVES 4

My mom made a few non-Italian dishes for us when we were growing up. Spanish rice and Jewish coffee cake are two I remember well. This recipe is a combination of the Spanish rice she sometimes used to stuff peppers and some suggestions given by those of our staff who grew up in Mexico.

    4 cups cooked brown rice
      Corn kernels cut from 3 ears, or one 10-ounce box frozen kernels
½ small red onion, diced
½ of a 10-ounce box frozen green peas
    1 large, ripe tomato, diced
    1 teaspoon chili powder
    2 tablespoons minced cilantro or parsley
      Salt and black pepper to taste
    3 tablespoons olive oil
    4 red bell peppers, cut in half lengthwise and seeded
    2 cups Salsa (see page 164)

Preheat the oven to 425 degrees. In a large bowl, combine the cooked rice, corn, onion, peas, tomato, chili powder, cilantro or parsley, salt, pepper, and olive oil. Mix well. Taste for seasoning. Mound about ½ cup of the stuffing in each pepper half. Arrange the peppers in a single layer in a large baking pan. Spoon ¼ cup Salsa over each pepper half. Pour enough water around (not on) the peppers to fill the pan to ½ inch. Cover the pan with foil. Bake for 30 minutes, then remove the foil and continue baking about 30 minutes, until the peppers are tender and the tops are nicely browned.

Entrees

This section offers a wide sampling of the recipes we prepare for dinner at **Claire's.** We serve our entrees with a cup of soup or a tossed salad and a little loaf of our homemade bread. Many of our customers order a half portion of several entrees, maybe Ratatouille with Risotto, or Lentils, Brown Rice, and Spinach, with Roasted Vegetables. At home, when I have the time, I like to prepare half portions of two or three different entrees for dinner. This provides the balance of nutrients, tastes, and textures we look forward to in our home-cooked meals.

Most of these entrees can be made ahead and frozen for the following week, which can be a big help for those of us with busy schedules.

Once you and your family see and taste the results of cooking a variety of homemade meatless meals, exploring the vast diversity of vegetables, grains, pastas, and beans, you'll grow to appreciate the time spent on cooking. As with every other task, organization is the key to success. Read through the recipes you plan to cook, checking your kitchen for the necessary ingredients. Prepare a grocery list, but be flexible, as many variables determine the quality and availability of fresh produce. Each week, you can buy your fresh fruits and vegetables according to which ones are in season and look best at the market. You might be dazzled by a perfect bunch of broccoli rabe and want to cook some with linguine, or you may be stopped by plump, fragrant strawberries, perfect for strawberry bread. Staples such as olive oil, soybean or vegetable oil, canned Italian whole peeled tomatoes, assorted pastas, brown rice, couscous (found at health-food stores and in the rice section of many large supermarkets), various dried beans, barley, oats, corn-

meal, flours, dried herbs and spices, and frozen green peas are items you should always keep on hand. If you include garlic, onions, parsley, and potatoes on your list of staples, you'll be on your way to many wonderful meals.

Stuffed Peppers 1

Serves 4

Eggplant has become very popular over the years, which makes us happy at **Claire's** because we love to cook with it. This recipe uses eggplant to stuff peppers. You can prepare the peppers up to two days in advance and refrigerate them until you're ready to bake them. They are even delicious served cold, which makes them good for a picnic.

3 tablespoons olive oil
1 large eggplant, chopped
4 cloves garlic, minced
1 small yellow onion, chopped
1 large tomato, chopped
  Salt to taste
¼ cup water
1 cup bread crumbs
¼ cup chopped fresh basil
¼ cup chopped flat-leaf parsley
¼ cup grated Parmesan
4 ounces grated mozzarella
  Black pepper to taste
4 bell peppers (red, yellow, green, or a combination), halved lengthwise and
    seeded
1 cup water

Preheat the oven to 400 degrees. Heat the olive oil in a large skillet over medium-low heat. Add the eggplant, garlic, onion, and tomato. Sprinkle with salt. Cover and cook, stirring frequently, for 10 minutes. Add the ¼ cup water and continue cooking, stirring frequently, until the eggplant is tender, about 25 minutes. Remove from the heat. Stir in the bread crumbs, basil, parsley, Parmesan, mozzarella, and pepper. Mix well. Taste for seasoning.

Divide the stuffing among the pepper halves. Arrange in a single layer in a rectangular glass baking dish. Pour the cup of water into the dish. Cover with foil. Bake for 45 minutes to 1 hour, until the peppers are tender when tested with a fork.

Stuffed Peppers II

SERVES 4

This stuffing of bread and mushrooms is wonderful baked in pepper halves. At home I often cut leftover halves into thirds and include them on an appetizer platter. They are delicious served hot or cold.

One 8-ounce loaf Italian or French bread
4 large cloves garlic, minced
¼ cup extra-virgin olive oil
¼ cup finely chopped flat-leaf parsley
1 pound white mushrooms, chopped
6 ounces fontina or mozzarella, diced
Salt and black pepper to taste
4 yellow bell peppers, cut in half lengthwise and seeded
1 cup water

Preheat the oven to 400 degrees. Tear the bread into pieces. Place in a colander and run under hot water for 30 seconds. Let stand until the bread is cool enough to handle, and squeeze out as much excess water as you can with your hands. Turn into a mixing bowl. Add the garlic, olive oil, parsley, mushrooms, cheese, salt, and pepper. Mix well. Taste for seasoning.

Divide the stuffing among the pepper halves. Arrange the pepper halves in a single layer in a rectangular glass baking dish. Pour in the water. Cover with foil and bake for 45 minutes to 1 hour, until the peppers are tender when tested with a fork.

Sweet and White Potato Pancakes

SERVES 4

My grandmother in New Haven made terrific potato pancakes. She served them with her homemade applesauce, and I ate them hot off the dish before they ever reached the table. If you do have leftovers, they are delicious eaten cold from the refrigerator. At **Claire's,** we sell as many as we make as often as we make them. We serve them with applesauce and low-fat sour cream.

    2 large white potatoes, peeled and grated
    1 large sweet potato, peeled and grated
    1 small onion, minced
    3 tablespoons finely chopped parsley
    3 eggs, beaten
      Salt and black pepper to taste
    ¼ cup plain bread crumbs
    ¼ cup unbleached flour
    ¼ to ½ cup soybean or vegetable oil for frying

Place the grated white and sweet potatoes in a colander. Press out as much liquid as you can with your hands. Turn into a bowl. Stir in the onion, parsley, eggs, salt, pepper, bread crumbs, and flour, combining well. Heat the oil in a nonstick skillet over medium heat. Test by dropping in a pinch of batter. When it quickly rises to the top, you can begin frying. Drop heaping tablespoons of the batter into the hot oil. Do not crowd the pan or the pancakes will be oily. Cook each side until golden brown, about 2 minutes. Turn each pancake carefully. Transfer the cooked pancakes to a double thickness of paper towels to drain while you fry the remaining batter.

Corn Fritters

SERVES 4

These fritters are very popular at **Claire's**. Over the years we have tried adding a variety of fresh herbs and spices to the batter, but our customers have always preferred the basic recipe, which allows the delicate fresh flavor of the corn to come through. When fresh corn is unavailable, we use frozen corn, and it works well. Serve these fritters hot or cold, with applesauce, honey, or low-fat sour cream.

> Corn kernels cut from 3 ears, or one 10-ounce box frozen kernels
> 1 cup unbleached flour
> 1 teaspoon baking powder
> Salt and black pepper to taste
> 2 eggs, beaten
> ½ cup milk
> 1 teaspoon olive oil
> ½ cup soybean or vegetable oil for frying

Cook the corn in boiling water about 3 minutes, until crisp-tender. Drain and set aside. In a bowl, whisk together the flour, baking powder, salt, and pepper. In a separate bowl, whisk together the eggs, milk, and olive oil until blended. Pour the liquid ingredients over the dry ingredients all at once. Mix with a spoon until combined. Stir in the corn.

Heat the soybean or vegetable oil in a large skillet over medium-low heat. The oil is ready for frying when a pinch of batter dropped in quickly rises to the top. Drop heaping tablespoons of the batter into the oil. Do not crowd the skillet or the fritters will be oily. Cook each side until golden brown, 2 or 3 minutes. Drain the fritters on a double thickness of paper towels while you fry the remaining batter.

Zucchini Fritters

SERVES 4

We make these fritters year-round at **Claire's.** During the summer months, when zucchini is grown locally, we are sometimes lucky enough to find a farmer who will give us the blossoms from the zucchini plants. We chop a few blossoms and add them to the batter, and they are heavenly. The tender orange blossoms add a delicate flavor.

> 4 cups grated unpeeled zucchini
> 2 eggs, lightly beaten
> ¼ cup chopped flat-leaf parsley
> 1 tablespoon grated lemon zest
> 4 or 5 squash blossoms, chopped (optional)
> 2 tablespoons grated Parmesan
> 1 cup unbleached flour
> 1 teaspoon baking powder
> Salt and black pepper to taste
> ½ cup soybean or vegetable oil for frying

In a bowl, combine the zucchini, eggs, parsley, lemon zest, squash blossoms if using, Parmesan, flour, baking powder, salt, and pepper. Beat lightly with a spoon to combine. Heat the oil in a large nonstick skillet over medium-low heat, until a pinch of batter dropped in rises quickly to the top. Drop heaping tablespoons of the batter into the skillet. Don't crowd the pan or the fritters will be oily. Cook each side of the fritters until golden brown, 2 or 3 minutes. Drain the cooked fritters on a double thickness of paper towels while you fry the remaining batter. Serve with lemon wedges or heated Marinara Sauce (see page 127).

Eggplant Roasted with Tomatoes

SERVES 6

My mother-in-law, who is a marvelous cook, loves eggplant and uses it in many excellent dishes. She often inspires me to try her recipes at **Claire's.** This is one of my favorites, served over spinach fettuccine, brown rice, or polenta.

    2 medium eggplants, unpeeled, sliced into ¾-inch rounds
    3 large tomatoes, sliced into ½-inch pieces
    ¼ cup extra-virgin olive oil
    4 cloves garlic, chopped
    ½ cup chopped fresh basil
    ½ cup chopped flat-leaf parsley
    2 tablespoons capers, rinsed
    2 tablespoons fresh rosemary leaves or 2 teaspoons dried rosemary
      Salt and black pepper to taste
    ⅓ cup hot water

Preheat the oven to 400 degrees. In a rectangular glass baking dish, alternate slices of eggplant and tomato, overlapping, in 2 rows. Drizzle with the olive oil. Over the eggplant and tomato slices scatter the garlic, basil, parsley, capers, and rosemary. Sprinkle with salt and pepper. Pour the hot water around (not on) the eggplant and tomatoes. Cover the dish tightly with foil. Bake for 45 minutes, or until the eggplant is as tender as you like it when pierced with a fork. Taste for seasoning.

Kim's Zucchini Casserole

SERVES 6

My sister-in-law Kim comes from a traditional meat-and-potatoes background, but she prepared this meatless one-dish meal at a cookout. Everyone loved the casserole, and the next day I made it at **Claire's.** I added a layer of cooked brown rice to Kim's recipe for increased nutrition.

> One 28-ounce can whole peeled tomatoes, crushed with your hands
> 3 tablespoons olive oil
> Salt and black pepper to taste
> 5 or 6 fresh basil leaves, chopped, or 1 teaspoon dried basil
> 2 cloves garlic, minced
> 2 cups cooked brown rice
> 2 medium zucchini, sliced into ½-inch rounds
> ¼ cup bread crumbs
> 3 tablespoons grated Parmesan
> 4 ounces shredded Monterey Jack cheese
> 1 medium yellow onion, sliced

Preheat the oven to 375 degrees. In a bowl, combine the tomatoes, olive oil, salt and pepper, basil, and garlic. Taste for seasoning. Spread the cooked brown rice evenly on the bottom of a rectangular glass baking dish. Spoon a little of the tomato mixture over the rice. Arrange a layer of half of the zucchini slices over the rice, overlapping them slightly. Sprinkle with bread crumbs, Parmesan, and Monterey Jack. Spoon a little sauce over the top. Scatter the onion slices evenly over the casserole. Arrange another layer of zucchini, and top with the remaining sauce. Bake the casserole, uncovered, about 1½ hours, or until the vegetables are tender when tested with a fork.

My Mom's Zucchini Bake

SERVES 6

My mom's friend Annette gave her a version of this recipe. I say a version, because they had a bad telephone connection while Mom was writing down the recipe. When Annette tasted the finished dish the next day, she was pleasantly surprised by the lovely orange flavor, but said she couldn't take credit for it as her recipe didn't call for orange juice (or parsley). This zucchini bake is an easy-to-make and easy-to-clean-up dish your family will enjoy. We sometimes serve it with Marinara Sauce (see page 127).

   2 medium zucchini, diced (about 5 cups)
   3 cups Bisquick baking mix
   ¼ cup grated Parmesan
   1 small yellow onion, chopped
   ¼ cup minced flat-leaf parsley
   ¼ cup chopped fresh basil
   2 cups cooked brown rice
   ¼ cup olive oil
   1 clove garlic, minced
   1 tablespoon freshly grated orange zest
     Juice of 1 orange
   6 eggs, lightly beaten
     Salt and black pepper to taste

Preheat the oven to 375 degrees. Combine all the ingredients in a large bowl and mix well with a spoon. Spray a rectangular glass baking dish with nonstick cooking spray. Turn the zucchini mixture into the dish. Bake for 55 minutes, or until the center feels set when touched with the back of a spoon. Cut into serving pieces using a metal spatula.

Stir-Fried Veggies Over Brown Rice

SERVES 4

We prepare a combination of stir-fried vegetables every day at **Claire's,** depending on the selection from the farmers' market. Choose your favorite vegetables of the season. When we want a change, we serve our stir-fries on a bed of couscous (a North African grain found in most supermarkets) instead of rice—either way it's a healthful, appealing meal.

¼ cup sesame oil
3 cloves garlic, chopped
1 teaspoon crushed red pepper flakes
One 1-inch piece fresh ginger, peeled and minced, or 2 teaspoons ground ginger
1 small red onion, chopped
2 medium carrots, cut into large matchsticks
¼ small green cabbage, chopped
1 small bunch broccoli, stems separated from florets, then chopped
1 small yellow bell pepper, cut in half, seeded, then sliced into ¼-inch ribs.
¼ cup chopped walnuts (optional)
¼ cup low-sodium soy sauce or tamari
2 tablespoons bottled mango chutney (found in the condiment section of most supermarkets) or honey
Salt and black pepper to taste
3 cups cooked brown rice

Heat the oil in a large skillet over medium-high heat. Add the garlic, red pepper flakes, ginger, and onion. Cook, stirring frequently, until the onion softens, about 5 minutes. Add the carrots, cabbage, broccoli stems only, and bell pepper. Cook, stirring frequently, until the vegetables are crisp-tender, about 10 minutes. Add the walnuts if using, broccoli florets, soy sauce or tamari, and chutney or honey. Continue cooking, stirring frequently, for 3 minutes. Taste for seasoning. Add salt and pepper to taste. Spread the cooked brown rice in a large serving dish. Spoon the stir-fried veggies and their juices evenly over the rice.

Oven-Roasted Potatoes and Peas

SERVES 4

This combination is one of my favorite dishes. The aroma of the roasting herbs will fill your kitchen and entice your family as it entices our customers, who love this cholesterol-free, protein- and vitamin-rich entree.

> 8 large red potatoes, sliced into ½-inch rounds
> 1 large yellow onion, chopped
> 4 cloves garlic, chopped
> ¼ cup olive oil
> 1 tablespoon chopped fresh rosemary or 1 teaspoon dried rosemary
> 1 tablespoon fresh thyme or ½ teaspoon dried thyme
> 1 tablespoon chopped fresh oregano or ½ teaspoon dried oregano
> 1 teaspoon paprika
> Salt and black pepper to taste
> Juice of 1 lemon
> One 10-ounce box frozen green peas

Preheat the oven to 425 degrees. In a large bowl, combine the potatoes, onion, garlic, olive oil, rosemary, thyme, oregano, paprika, salt, and pepper. Toss well. Turn into a rectangular glass baking dish. Bake for 45 minutes, stirring once after 20 minutes, until the potatoes are tender. Remove from the oven and pour the lemon juice evenly over the top of the potatoes. Add the green peas and stir to combine. Return to the oven and continue baking for 10 minutes.

Roasted Vegetables

SERVES 4

This lovely dish is delicious served in a variety of ways. We present it over brown rice, pasta with Marinara Sauce (see page 127), polenta, barley, or couscous. It makes a wonderful dinner any time of year, especially during the winter months, when you appreciate a warm kitchen.

3 small bell peppers (1 each red, yellow, and green), cut in half, seeded, then sliced into ½-inch ribs
3 baby Italian eggplants, each about 4 inches long, sliced into ½-inch rounds
1 medium tomato, chopped
2 large red potatoes, sliced into ½-inch rounds
1 small yellow onion, chopped
1 small zucchini, sliced into ½-inch rounds
1 small yellow squash, sliced into ½-inch rounds
3 cloves garlic, chopped
¼ cup chopped fresh basil leaves or ½ teaspoon dried basil
¼ cup olive oil
   Salt and black pepper to taste
3 tablespoons water

Preheat the oven to 400 degrees. In a large bowl, combine all the ingredients and toss well. Taste for seasoning. Turn into a rectangular glass baking pan. Sprinkle with the water. Cover tightly with foil. Bake for 45 minutes. Remove from the oven. Remove the foil and stir the vegetables. Return to the oven, uncovered, and continue baking for 15 minutes, until the eggplant is tender and all the vegetables are browned.

Stuffed Zucchini Boats

SERVES 4

We love these zucchini boats during the summers at **Claire's**, when local farmers practically give away their big-as-tenpins native zucchini. We slice the zucchini in half lengthwise, scoop out the seeds and some pulp, fill the cavities with our flavorful, colorful stuffing, and bake them until tender. They are marvelous hot from the oven or chilled, which makes them perfect to take along on a picnic.

    1 large zucchini, about 14 inches long
    ¼ cup olive oil
    ½ small red onion, diced
    1 medium red bell pepper, seeded and diced
      Fresh corn kernels cut from 1 ear, or ½ cup frozen kernels
    ¼ pound mushrooms, chopped
    4 cups cooked brown rice
    ¼ cup sliced black olives
    1 teaspoon dried mint
      Salt and black pepper to taste

Preheat the oven to 375 degrees. Cut the zucchini in half lengthwise. Scoop out the seeds and only as much pulp as necessary to create about a 1¾-inch cavity. Cut each half in half crosswise; you should have 4 pieces about 7 inches long. Set aside. Heat the olive oil in a large skillet over medium-low heat. Add the onion, pepper, and corn kernels. Cook about 10 minutes, stirring frequently. Add the mushrooms and continue cooking for 5 minutes, stirring frequently. Remove from the heat. Add the cooked rice, olives, mint, salt, and pepper. Stir to mix well. Taste for seasoning. Spoon the filling evenly into the zucchini shells. Arrange in a baking pan. Pour about 1 cup water into the pan and cover tightly with foil. Bake for 1½ hours, or until the zucchini are tender when pierced with a fork.

Curried Zucchini and Brown Rice Pilaf

SERVES 4

This is a marvelous dish, perfect any time of year, with a mild curry flavor, crunchy texture, and colorful appearance. I like it for a picnic, served slightly chilled.

   5 cups cooked brown rice
     Juice of 1 lemon
     Juice of 1 lime
½ cup chopped parsley
½ small ripe pineapple, cut into ½-inch cubes
   2 tablespoons bottled mango chutney (found in the condiment section of most supermarkets)
¼ cup olive oil
   1 large onion, chopped
One 1-inch piece fresh ginger, peeled and minced, or 1 teaspoon ground ginger
   1 tablespoon curry powder
   5 cups diced zucchini
   1 cup chopped walnuts
     Salt and black pepper to taste

In a bowl, combine the cooked rice, lemon and lime juices, parsley, pineapple, and chutney. Toss well. Set aside. Heat the olive oil in a large skillet over medium-low heat. Add the onion, ginger, and curry powder. Cook for 5 minutes, stirring frequently. Add the zucchini and continue cooking for 10 minutes, stirring frequently, until crisp-tender. Stir in the walnuts. Add the rice mixture. Sprinkle with salt and pepper and stir to combine well. Cook for 2 minutes, or until heated through. Taste for seasoning.

Spinach-Noodle Kugel

SERVES 6

This traditional Jewish dish is popular at **Claire's**. We sometimes omit the noodles or replace them with thin slices of potatoes, precooked until they are crisp-tender.

> **One 10-ounce bag fresh spinach**
> **8 ounces low-fat cream cheese, cut into 8 pieces**
> **1 pound low-fat cottage cheese**
> **4 eggs, lightly beaten**
> **½ teaspoon nutmeg**
> **¼ pound thin egg noodles, cooked**
> **Salt and black pepper to taste**
> **¼ cup plain bread crumbs or matzoh meal**

Preheat the oven to 375 degrees. Soak the spinach in a bowl of warm water to cover for 1 minute. Lift the spinach from the water to a colander, using your hands, allowing any sand to remain on the bottom of the bowl. Transfer the spinach and any water clinging to the leaves to a pot. Cover and cook over medium-low heat about 5 minutes, until wilted. Check often to prevent the leaves from burning. Remove from the heat. Add the cream cheese and stir until the cream cheese has melted from the heat of the spinach. Stir in the cottage cheese, eggs, nutmeg, noodles, salt, and pepper. Beat with a spoon until well mixed.

Spray a 2-quart rectangular glass baking dish with nonstick cooking spray. Turn the mixture into the baking dish and sprinkle with the bread crumbs or matzoh meal. Bake about 45 minutes, or until the center is set and somewhat firm.

Lentils, Brown Rice, and Spinach

SERVES 6

Lentils and rice were always a welcome combination at our house. My mom still uses a lot of lentils in her cooking. We love their delicious flavor, and we like knowing that lentils are rich in protein and iron and are also fat-free. At **Claire's,** we often use 20 or more pounds a week.

> 1 pound lentils, picked over
> 3 quarts water
> 1 cup brown rice, uncooked
> 2 bay leaves
> 1 cup chopped flat-leaf parsley
> ¼ cup olive oil
> 4 large cloves garlic, chopped
> One 10-ounce bag fresh spinach, rinsed well and chopped
> ½ cup chopped fresh basil
> Salt and black pepper to taste
> Grated Romano (optional)

Put the lentils and water in a large pot. Cover and bring to a boil over high heat. Stir in the brown rice, bay leaves, and parsley. Lower the heat to medium and cook, uncovered, stirring frequently, until the beans and rice are very soft, about 1¼ hours. Keep the mixture warm. In a large skillet, heat the olive oil over medium-low heat. Add the garlic. Cook, stirring frequently, for 3 minutes, until softened but not brown. Add the spinach, basil, salt, and pepper. Cover and cook for 5 to 10 minutes, stirring occasionally, until the spinach is wilted. Add the spinach mixture to the lentils and stir to combine. Taste for seasoning. Serve with plenty of good bread for dunking, and sprinkle with grated Romano if desired.

Curried Eggplant and Potato in Flour Tortillas (Rotie)

SERVES 6

This recipe was inspired by Shannon Murphy, one of the most creative cooks ever to work at **Claire's.** During a vacation, Shannon enjoyed a West Indian *rotie* of curried meat baked in a turnover. She knew how much I love curries and suggested I try a vegetarian version, and after some trials, I came up with this recipe. We fill a large flour tortilla instead of pastry dough, and serve the *rotie* with plain yogurt mixed with a little chutney.

    5 large potatoes, cut in half, then each half cut into eighths
    ¼ cup olive oil
    1 large onion, chopped
    1 medium eggplant, unpeeled, chopped
    1 tablespoon curry powder
      Pinch cayenne pepper or more to taste
      Salt and black pepper to taste
    ¼ cup bottled mango chutney (found in the condiment section of most
        supermarkets)
  Six 10-inch flour tortillas

Topping:

    1½ cups plain nonfat yogurt
    2 tablespoons bottled mango chutney

Cook the potatoes in boiling water about 10 minutes, or until just tender. Drain, reserving ¼ cup of the cooking liquid, and set aside. Heat the olive oil in a large skillet over medium-low heat. Add the onion and eggplant. Sprinkle with the curry powder, cayenne pepper, salt, and black pepper. Cover and cook for 15 minutes, stirring frequently. If the eggplant begins to stick, lower the heat. Add the reserved cooking liquid from the potatoes and continue cooking, cov-

ered, stirring frequently, about 30 minutes, until the eggplant is tender. Add the potatoes and chutney and mix to combine well. Continue cooking for 5 minutes, stirring frequently. Taste for seasoning. Remove from the heat and set aside.

Preheat the oven to 375 degrees. Spray 2 cookie sheets with nonstick cooking spray or line with parchment paper. To assemble the *rotie,* arrange the flour tortillas in a single layer on the prepared cookie sheets. Divide the filling among the tortillas, spooning a line of filling along the middle of each tortilla. Fold one side of the tortilla over the filling, then fold the other side over and gently turn the tortillas seam side down on the cookie sheets. Bake until the tortillas are golden brown, about 10 minutes.

Meanwhile, prepare the topping by mixing the yogurt and chutney in a bowl. Arrange the *rotie* on a serving platter and spoon ¼ cup topping over the top of each.

Eggplant with Mascarpone

SERVES 4

Mascarpone is a soft and creamy, slightly sweet Italian cheese, found in Italian import stores or gourmet delis. Most people associate it with *tiramisu*, the fabulous rich Italian dessert. But if you use mascarpone only for dessert, you will be missing out. It is marvelous with eggplant. If you cannot locate mascarpone, you can substitute whipped cream cheese, and although it is not the same, the finished dish will still taste delicious.

> ½ cup flour or more for dredging the eggplant
> 3 eggs
> 2 tablespoons chopped flat-leaf parsley
> 2 tablespoons grated Parmesan
> Salt and black pepper to taste
> ¼ cup soybean or vegetable oil for frying
> 1 medium eggplant, peeled and sliced lengthwise into ¼-inch rounds
> 4 cups Marinara Sauce (see page 127)
> 8 ounces mascarpone or whipped cream cheese
> 15 to 20 spinach leaves, rinsed, drained, tough stems removed

Put the flour in a shallow bowl and set aside. Lightly beat the eggs in a bowl. Add the parsley and Parmesan. Sprinkle lightly with salt and pepper and beat lightly. Heat the oil in a large nonstick skillet over medium-low heat. Dredge each slice of eggplant, one at a time, in flour to coat. Shake off the excess. Dip each eggplant slice into the eggs to coat. Shake off the excess. Place the slice in the hot oil. Repeat with as many slices as will fit in a single layer without crowding the skillet. Cook the slices for 1 or 2 minutes, until golden brown. Carefully turn and brown the other sides. Drain the slices on a cookie sheet lined with a double thickness of paper towels. Repeat the process with the remaining eggplant slices, heating additional oil if needed. Set aside until cool enough to handle.

Preheat the oven to 350 degrees. Pour the Marinara Sauce into a rectangular glass baking dish. Hold one eggplant slice in your hand and spoon a heaping tablespoon of mascarpone onto one half of the eggplant. Place 1 or 2 spinach

leaves on top of the cheese. Fold the top half of the eggplant slice over the filling, pressing lightly to hold together. Set the eggplant sandwich on the Marinara
Sauce and repeat the process until all the eggplant slices are filled and arranged
in a single layer on the sauce. Bake about 30 minutes, until the sauce and cheese
are heated through.

Risotto Milanese

SERVES 4

This is a delicious dish, although untraditional in that we have substituted short-grain brown rice for arborio rice, and our version is easier and quicker to prepare than the labor-intensive traditional risotto. This meal is also easy to make ahead, which cannot be said for traditional risotto.

> 2 carrots, diced
> 2 small zucchini, diced
> 1 small yellow squash, diced
> 2 cups short-grain brown rice, uncooked
>   Pinch saffron threads
> ½ pound mushrooms, sliced
> ½ cup Marsala
> ¼ cup olive oil
> 2 cloves garlic, minced
> 1 small red onion, chopped
> 1 red bell pepper, seeded and diced
>   Salt and black pepper to taste
> ¼ cup chopped flat-leaf parsley
> One 10-ounce box frozen green peas
> ¼ cup grated Parmesan
> ¼ cup chopped walnuts
> 4 ounces shredded mozzarella (optional)

Boil the carrots, zucchini, and yellow squash in enough water to cover by 2 inches. Cook about 5 minutes, or until crisp-tender. Drain the vegetables, reserving the cooking liquid. Add enough water to the cooking liquid to measure 5 cups. Pour into a large pot. Add the rice and saffron. Cover and bring to a boil over medium-high heat. Lower the heat and simmer, covered, about 35 minutes, or until the rice is tender and the water is absorbed.

Meanwhile, preheat the oven to 350 degrees. Place the mushrooms and Marsala in a bowl. Toss lightly to coat. Set aside. Heat the olive oil in a skillet over medium-low heat. Add the garlic, onion, and bell pepper. Sprinkle lightly with salt and pepper. Cook for 10 minutes, stirring frequently, until crisp-tender. Stir in the parsley and peas. Cook for 5 minutes, stirring frequently. Turn into a large bowl. Add the cooked rice, vegetables, and mushrooms, including their liquid, and the Parmesan, walnuts, and mozzarella if using. Stir to mix well. Turn into a baking dish and bake for 20 minutes.

Stuffed Acorn Squash 1

SERVES 4

This is one of my favorite fall and winter meals. The combination of savory and sweet is marvelous. I often serve this "roast" on holidays and other festive occasions. The flavor of the meatless sausage is incredibly good, and it contains no cholesterol. You can find Light Life brand Lean Links Italian Sausage (that's the brand I use) in the frozen-food section of most health-food stores. Serve this stuffed squash with mashed potatoes and spinach and warm cranberry sauce for a memorable meal.

> ½ of a 12-ounce package tofu sausage, cut into small pieces
> 2 cups water
> ½ stick margarine (I prefer soy margarine, found in health-food stores)
> 1 medium yellow onion, chopped
> 6 stalks celery, finely chopped
> ½ teaspoon dried thyme
> ½ teaspoon dried sage
> One 6-ounce bag or box plain stuffing cubes
> Salt and black pepper to taste
> ½ cup unsweetened applesauce
> 1 small Granny Smith apple, peeled and diced
> ¼ cup apple cider
> 2 large acorn squash, cut in half and seeded

Preheat the oven to 450 degrees. Brown the pieces of tofu sausage in a nonstick skillet coated with a little olive oil. Set aside. Bring the water and margarine to a boil in a covered pot. Stir in the onion, celery, thyme, and sage. Cook, covered, stirring frequently, for 3 minutes. Remove from the heat. Stir in the stuffing cubes, salt and pepper, applesauce, apple, and cider; combine well. Stir in the cooked tofu sausage and combine well. Taste for seasoning.

Divide the stuffing evenly among the acorn squash halves. Arrange the halves in a roasting pan and pour water into the pan to 1 inch. Cover the pan tightly with foil. Bake about 1½ hours, until the squash is tender when pierced with a fork.

Stuffed Acorn Squash II

SERVES 4

We use a blend of wild and brown rice to enhance the flavor and give an interesting texture to this aromatic dish.

¼ cup olive oil
2 cloves garlic, minced
1 small red onion, finely chopped
4 ribs celery, minced
1 small zucchini, diced
¼ pound mushrooms, chopped
½ of a 10-ounce box frozen green peas
½ teaspoon dried rosemary
½ teaspoon dried sage
5 cups cooked wild and brown rice
Salt and black pepper to taste
¼ cup chopped pecans
4 ounces shredded Monterey Jack cheese
2 large acorn squash, cut in half and seeded

Preheat the oven to 450 degrees. Heat the olive oil in a large skillet over medium-low heat. Add the garlic, onion, and celery. Cook for 5 minutes, stirring frequently. Add the zucchini, mushrooms, peas, rosemary, and sage. Cook for 5 minutes, stirring frequently, until softened. Stir in the cooked rice, salt and pepper, and pecans. Combine well. Remove from the heat. Stir in the cheese and combine well. Taste for seasoning.

Divide the stuffing evenly among the squash halves. Arrange the halves in a baking pan and pour water into the pan to 1 inch. Cover the pan tightly with foil. Bake for 1½ hours, or until the squash is tender when pierced with a fork.

Moroccan Sweet Potatoes

SERVES 6

Everyone knows how rich in beta-carotene sweet potatoes and carrots are, and this delicious, sweet combination also contains chickpeas for protein and additional fiber. This recipe is based on a traditional Moroccan dish of meat roasted with sweet potatoes, chickpeas, and raisins. Our customers love our cholesterol-free version.

        6 medium sweet potatoes, cut into 1-inch cubes
        3 medium carrots, cut on the diagonal into ½-inch slices
        1 large yellow onion, sliced into ¼-inch rings
     ¼ cup olive oil
        1 teaspoon cinnamon
     ¼ cup brown sugar
        1 tablespoon vanilla extract
     ¼ cup golden raisins
        Salt and black pepper to taste
     ⅓ cup water
    One 16-ounce can chickpeas
     ¼ cup chopped walnuts

Preheat the oven to 400 degrees. In a large bowl, combine the sweet potatoes, carrots, onion, olive oil, cinnamon, brown sugar, vanilla extract, and raisins. Sprinkle lightly with salt and pepper. Toss well. Pour the water into a rectangular glass baking dish. Turn the potato mixture into the dish. Cover tightly with foil. Bake for 1 hour. Remove the foil and stir in the chickpeas and walnuts. Continue cooking, uncovered, for 10 minutes, until the potatoes are tender.

Curried Couscous

SERVES 4

Couscous is a flavorful, light grain made from semolina. I was introduced to this pasta-like ingredient by Debbie Rhine, an employee at **Claire's** during the late seventies. Debbie's original couscous led to many exciting variations; this is one of our most popular. It has a light curry flavor and an extra-healthful combination of vegetables, beans, and grains.

6 cups water
2 tablespoons butter, margarine, or olive oil
1 small yellow onion, sliced into thin rings
4 ribs celery, diced
2 carrots, cut into matchsticks
2 medium potatoes, peeled and diced
2 teaspoons curry powder
2 tablespoons mango chutney (found in the condiment section of most
    supermarkets), optional
1 cup cooked or canned chickpeas
¼ cup golden raisins
1 apple (such as Macintosh or Rome), diced
    Salt and black pepper to taste
2 cups couscous (found in the rice section of most supermarkets and health-
    food stores)

Bring the water to a boil in a large covered pot. Add the butter, margarine, or olive oil, onion, celery, carrots, potatoes, curry powder, and chutney, if desired. Lower the heat to medium and simmer, covered, for 30 minutes, stirring frequently, until softened to your liking. Stir in the cooked chickpeas, raisins, apple, salt, and pepper and combine well. Stir in the couscous and mix well. Remove from the heat, cover, and let stand for 5 minutes. Fluff with two forks. Taste for seasoning.

Eggplant Balls

Serves 4

My grandmother in Bridgeport often added cooked eggplant and raisins to her meatballs. I always loved the interesting combination of flavors, and when I began to eliminate meat from my diet I searched for new ways to enjoy such favorite foods. These little gems are marvelous served a variety of ways. You can enjoy them baked with Marinara Sauce (see page 127) and mozzarella, alone or on a grinder (sub sandwich) roll, or on top of spaghetti with Marinara Sauce. I like to make little eggplant balls and serve them as an appetizer with warm Marinara Sauce for dipping.

    ¼ cup olive oil
    3 cloves garlic, minced
    2 large eggplants, peeled and diced
    2 tablespoons water
    2 cups bread crumbs
    ½ cup chopped flat-leaf parsley
    2 tablespoons chopped fresh basil leaves
    4 ounces shredded mozzarella (optional)
    4 eggs, lightly beaten
    ¼ cup grated Parmesan
      Salt and black pepper to taste
    ½ cup flour or more for rolling the eggplant balls
      Soybean or vegetable oil for frying (optional)

Heat the olive oil in a large skillet over medium-low heat. Add the garlic and cook for 1 minute, stirring frequently, until softened. Add the diced eggplant and stir to coat. Add the water, cover, and cook about 20 minutes, stirring frequently, until the eggplant is very soft. Remove from the heat and turn into a bowl. Add the bread crumbs, parsley, basil, mozzarella if using, eggs, Parmesan, salt, and pepper. Stir to mix well. Taste for seasoning. Let the mixture stand for 15 minutes.

Form the mixture into balls, bite-sized for appetizers or larger for entrees. Carefully place the balls on a cookie sheet while you form the rest. Measure

about ½ cup flour into a shallow bowl. Gently roll each ball in the flour to coat evenly.

To fry the balls, heat the soybean or vegetable oil in a large nonstick skillet over medium heat. Arrange the balls in the hot oil, allowing a little space in between. Fry each side about 1 minute, until golden brown, turning carefully. Drain on a cookie sheet lined with a double thickness of paper towels while you fry the remaining balls. Heat additional oil if necessary.

If you prefer, you can bake the balls in a preheated 350-degree oven about 30 minutes, turning once after 15 minutes.

Szechwan-Style Eggplant

SERVES 4

This eggplant and carrot dish is my interpretation of the hot and spicy Szechwan vegetables I've enjoyed at Chinese restaurants. It's just marvelous for all who enjoy fire in their food. Serve it over brown rice or soba (buckwheat) noodles, which can be found in most health-food stores.

 ¼ cup olive oil
 4 cloves garlic, chopped
 1 teaspoon crushed red pepper flakes
   Pinch cayenne pepper
 2 medium eggplants, cut into 4-x-1-inch spears
 3 carrots, cut on the diagonal into ½-inch slices
 2 teaspoons cornstarch
 2 tablespoons tamari or soy sauce
 ¼ cup red-wine vinegar
   Salt and black pepper to taste

Heat the oil in a large skillet over medium-low heat. Add the garlic, red pepper flakes, cayenne pepper, and eggplant. Cover and cook over low heat for 30 minutes, stirring frequently. Add the carrots and continue cooking, covered, for 20 minutes, until the eggplant is tender and the carrots are crisp-tender. Put the cornstarch in a separate bowl. Whisk in the tamari or soy sauce and vinegar. Whisk until smooth. Pour the cornstarch mixture all at once into the skillet, stirring to combine well. Sprinkle with salt and pepper. Cook uncovered, stirring frequently, for 3 minutes, until the mixture thickens. Taste for seasoning.

Italian Vegetable Stew

SERVES 6

There's nothing like a hearty stew for flavor and variety. Each season brings us a healthful selection of vegetables to choose from. Serve your stew with plenty of good bread for mopping up the juices or over brown rice.

¼ cup plus 2 tablespoons olive oil
1 small yellow onion
4 cloves garlic, chopped
2 medium carrots, chopped
6 ribs celery, chopped
1 small head cauliflower, cored and chopped into 2-inch lengths
2 large red potatoes, cut into 1-inch pieces
½ cup chopped flat-leaf parsley
Two 28-ounce cans Italian whole peeled tomatoes, crushed with your hands
¼ cup water
½ teaspoon dried oregano
2 bay leaves
One 10-ounce box frozen green peas
¼ cup chopped fresh basil
Salt and black pepper to taste

Heat the oil in a large heavy pot over low heat. Add the onion and garlic. Cover and cook for 10 minutes, stirring frequently. Add the carrots, celery, cauliflower, potatoes, and parsley. Cook, covered, over low heat for 15 minutes, stirring frequently. Add the tomatoes, water, oregano, and bay leaves. Raise the heat to medium-low. Cook, covered, for 45 minutes to 1 hour, stirring frequently, until tender. Stir in the peas, basil, salt, and pepper. Continue cooking for 10 minutes, stirring frequently, until the peas are heated through. Taste for seasoning.

Ratatouille

SERVES 6

This is my mom's recipe for ratatouille, and it's the best I've ever had. Although we enjoy this dish year-round, we take extra pleasure in preparing it during summer when our incomparable native produce is so abundant.

    3 large red potatoes, cut into 1-inch pieces
    6 tablespoons olive oil
    4 cloves garlic, chopped
    1 large eggplant, cut into 1-inch cubes
    2 tablespoons water
      Salt and black pepper to taste
    ½ cup coarsely chopped fresh basil
    ¼ cup coarsely chopped flat-leaf parsley
    1 medium yellow onion, cut into 1-inch pieces
    4 bell peppers (yellow, red, and green), seeded and cut into ½-inch ribs
    3 large, ripe tomatoes, cut into 1-inch pieces
    2 medium zucchini, cut into 1-inch pieces
    ½ pound mushrooms, thickly sliced
    ¼ cup sliced black olives

Cook the potatoes in lightly salted boiling water until crisp-tender. Drain and set aside. Heat 2 tablespoons of the olive oil in a large skillet over low heat. Add about half the chopped garlic. Cook for 3 minutes, stirring frequently. Add the eggplant and sprinkle with the water, salt, and pepper. Cover and cook for 30 minutes, stirring frequently, until tender. Stir in half the basil and the parsley. Remove from the heat. Turn the eggplant mixture into a large bowl and set aside. Carefully wipe the skillet clean.

Heat 2 tablespoons of the olive oil in the skillet over medium-low heat. Add the onion and cook, uncovered, for 5 minutes, stirring frequently. Stir in the peppers. Continue cooking for 15 minutes, stirring frequently, until the peppers are crisp-tender. Stir in the tomatoes and the remaining ¼ cup of basil. Continue

cooking for 10 minutes, stirring frequently, until tender. Remove from the heat. Add the cooked pepper mixture to the bowl of cooked eggplant and set aside. Carefully wipe the skillet clean.

Heat the remaining 2 tablespoons of the olive oil in the skillet over medium-low heat. Add the remaining garlic and cook for 2 minutes, stirring frequently. Add the zucchini and cook for 15 minutes, stirring frequently, until crisp-tender. Add the mushrooms. Continue cooking, stirring frequently, for 10 minutes, until crisp-tender. Remove from the heat. Drain the juices and reserve for another use (such as vegetable soup). Return the drained zucchini mixture to the skillet. Add the reserved potatoes and the other cooked vegetables, and the olives. Stir gently but thoroughly to combine and heat through. Taste for seasoning.

Glazed Fall Vegetables

SERVES 4

Serve this fragrant dish with a savory herb stuffing or rice, a mixed green salad, and warm cranberry sauce for a wonderful meal on a cold autumn night.

2 large sweet potatoes, sliced into ½-inch pieces
1 large white potato, sliced into ½-inch pieces
3 medium carrots, sliced into ½-inch pieces
1 small yellow onion, cut into ½-inch rings
1 medium acorn squash, halved, seeded, and peeled, each half cut into thirds
½ cup packed brown sugar
¼ cup pure maple syrup
1 teaspoon vanilla extract
1 teaspoon cinnamon
4 tablespoons (½ stick) butter or margarine, cut into 8 pieces
¼ cup water

Preheat the oven to 425 degrees. Place the sweet and white potatoes, carrots, onion, and acorn squash in a large bowl. Add the brown sugar, maple syrup, vanilla extract, and cinnamon. Toss well.

Turn into a rectangular glass baking dish. Scatter the butter or margarine pieces over the top. Pour the water into the baking dish. Cover tightly with foil and bake for 45 minutes. Remove the foil and stir the vegetables. Continue baking about 15 minutes, until the vegetables are softened to your liking and lightly browned.

Spaghetti Frittata

SERVES 6

I enjoy this frittata warm with Marinara Sauce (see page 127) for dinner, along with roasted potatoes. But I like it best the next day for breakfast with the left-over roasted potatoes and ketchup.

    ½ pound whole-wheat spaghetti, broken into 1-inch pieces
    12 eggs, lightly beaten
    ¼ cup grated Parmesan
    1 small onion, minced
    ½ cup ricotta
    ¼ cup minced parsley
    1 teaspoon black pepper
    4 ounces fontina, shredded
    ½ cup bread crumbs

Preheat the oven to 350 degrees. Cook the spaghetti according to the package directions. Drain, run under cold water, drain again, and turn into a bowl. Add the remaining ingredients, except the bread crumbs, and combine well.

Turn into an oiled rectangular glass baking dish. Sprinkle with the bread crumbs. Bake for 55 minutes, until the center is set. Let stand for 15 minutes before cutting into serving pieces.

Escarole Pie

SERVES 6

I discovered vegetable pies in New York, at a magnificent food shop on the Upper West Side. The shop had a beautiful pie with layers of fontina, prosciutto, roasted red peppers, and artichoke hearts. It was a lovely sight, and the next day at **Claire's** I made my version with layers of colorful vegetables. Vegetable pies are perfect for lunch or dinner, make a delightful brunch dish, and are among my favorite picnic foods. There are as many possible variations as there are vegetables and cheeses, so try all your favorites and have fun experimenting.

  ¼ **cup olive oil**
  6 **large cloves garlic, chopped**
  ¼ **cup black olives, chopped**
  1 **tablespoon capers, rinsed**
  2 **heads escarole, chopped**
  ½ **teaspoon crushed red pepper flakes**
  1 **teaspoon fennel seeds**
    Pastry for a 9-inch, 2-crust pie (a good store-bought pastry is fine)
  8 **ounces fresh mozzarella, diced**

Preheat the oven to 375 degrees. Heat the olive oil in a large skillet over medium heat. Add the garlic, olives, and capers. Cook for 5 minutes, stirring often. Do not let the garlic burn or it will taste bitter. Add the escarole, red pepper flakes, and fennel seeds. Cover, reduce the heat to low, and allow to steam 30 minutes, stirring frequently, until the escarole is tender. If it begins to stick, lower the heat. Stir to mix well. Taste for seasoning. Drain in a colander.

Sprinkle half the mozzarella over the bottom pie crust. Put the escarole mixture in the crust, spreading evenly. Sprinkle the remaining mozzarella over the top. Cover with the top pie crust, sealing the edges with the tines of a fork. Cut 3 slits in the crust to allow steam to escape. Bake for 45 minutes, until golden brown. Let stand for 15 minutes before cutting into wedges.

Roasted Baby Eggplant Halves

SERVES 6

These little eggplant halves are delicious and so easy to prepare that you'll love them as much as our customers do. We serve them with penne and Marinara Sauce (see page 127), a simple green salad, and bread.

- 6 baby Italian eggplants, each about 5 inches long, halved lengthwise
    Salt and black pepper to taste
- 3 ripe tomatoes, finely chopped
- 2 tablespoons capers, rinsed
- 4 cloves garlic, minced
- ¼ cup finely chopped black olives
- ¼ cup finely chopped fresh basil
- ½ teaspoon dried oregano
- ¼ cup olive oil
- 1 cup low-fat ricotta (optional)

Preheat the oven to 375 degrees. Using a sharp knife, carefully make slashes about halfway through the cut side of the eggplant halves. Arrange the eggplant halves, cut side up, in a baking pan. Sprinkle lightly with salt and pepper. Set aside.

In a separate bowl, combine the tomatoes, capers, garlic, olives, basil, oregano, and olive oil. Mix well. Taste for seasoning. Spoon the mixture evenly over the eggplant halves.

Pour hot water into the pan to ½ inch. Cover the pan tightly with foil. Bake for 1 hour, then remove the foil and, if using, spoon the ricotta evenly over the eggplant. Continue baking for 30 minutes, until the eggplant is tender.

Eggplant Casserole

SERVES 6

My mother-in-law makes some of the most delicious vegetable casseroles I've ever eaten, and I always look forward to dinner at her house. She has been a tremendous source of recipes for me and for **Claire's**. This is her ever-popular eggplant casserole, which we make at least once a week. You can serve it alone as an entree or with linguine and Marinara Sauce (see page 127).

> 1 medium eggplant, sliced into ¼-inch rounds
> Salt and black pepper to taste
> ¼ cup olive oil
> 4 cloves garlic, minced
> ½ cup bread crumbs
> ¼ cup grated Parmesan
> 8 ounces shredded mozzarella
> 4 medium potatoes, peeled and sliced into ¼-inch rounds
> 1 yellow bell pepper, seeded and cut into ½-inch ribs
> 1 red bell pepper, seeded and cut into ½-inch ribs
> 1 medium yellow onion, sliced into ¼-inch rings
> 1 medium zucchini, sliced into ½-inch rounds
> One 28-ounce can crushed tomatoes

Preheat the oven to 400 degrees. Arrange the eggplant slices on the bottom and along the sides of a rectangular glass baking dish. Sprinkle lightly with salt and pepper. Drizzle with 1 tablespoon of the olive oil, ¼ of the garlic, 2 tablespoons of the bread crumbs, 1 tablespoon of the grated Parmesan, and ¼ of the mozzarella. Arrange the sliced potatoes over the eggplant, overlapping slightly. Sprinkle lightly with salt and pepper. Sprinkle with ¼ of the garlic, 1 tablespoon of the bread crumbs, 1 tablespoon of the olive oil, 1 tablespoon of the Parmesan, and ¼ of the mozzarella. Arrange the bell peppers and onion rings over the top. Sprinkle with a little salt and pepper, ¼ of the garlic, 1 tablespoon of the bread crumbs, 1 tablespoon of the olive oil, 1 tablespoon of the Parmesan, and ¼ of the mozzarella. Arrange the zucchini over the top.

In a separate bowl, combine the crushed tomatoes, the remaining garlic and olive oil, and a little salt and pepper. Spoon over the casserole. Sprinkle with the remaining bread crumbs, Parmesan, and mozzarella. Cover tightly with foil. Bake for 1½ hours, then remove the foil and continue baking for 30 minutes, or until the vegetables are tender when tested with a fork.

Potato Croquettes

SERVES 4

When I was a child, my mom served massive quantities of delicious mashed potatoes with dinner at least once a week. She often had leftovers to make into wonderful croquettes that we enjoyed with the next night's dinner. Today at **Claire's** we serve them with either applesauce and low-fat sour cream or Marinara Sauce (see page 127).

    6 large red potatoes, quartered
    2 tablespoons butter
    2 tablespoons milk
    2 tablespoons chopped flat-leaf parsley
      Salt and black pepper to taste
    2 eggs
    1 cup bread crumbs
    ¼ cup or more olive oil for frying

Cook the potatoes in lightly salted boiling water until soft, about 20 minutes. Drain and turn into a bowl. Add the butter, milk, parsley, salt, and pepper. Thoroughly mash with a potato masher, mixing well. Taste for seasoning. Set aside until cool enough to handle.

Form ¼-cup measures of the mashed potatoes into cylinders about 2 inches × 4 inches. Arrange in a single layer on a cookie sheet and refrigerate until firm to the touch. Beat the eggs lightly in a bowl large enough to dip a croquette. Set aside. Measure the bread crumbs into a separate bowl. Set aside. Dip each croquette into the beaten eggs, turning to coat evenly, then shake off the excess and roll the croquette in the bread crumbs to coat evenly. Return to the cookie sheet while you repeat the process with the remaining croquettes.

Heat the oil in a large nonstick skillet over medium heat. Add as many croquettes as you can fit into the skillet without crowding. Brown all sides of the croquettes, about 1 minute per side, turning when golden brown. Heat additional oil if needed. Drain on a plate lined with a double thickness of paper towels.

Colcannon

SERVES 6

This is our traditional St. Patrick's Day special, although we also serve it at many other times because it is so good. The kale provides generous amounts of vitamins A and C, calcium, and iron.

    4 quarts water
1½ pounds kale, chopped into 2-inch pieces
    2 leeks, well washed and chopped (about 1½ cups)
    6 large potatoes, peeled, cut into eighths
    4 tablespoons (½ stick) butter, margarine, or soy margarine (available at most health-food stores)
¼ cup olive oil
    Salt and black pepper to taste

Bring the water to a boil in a large covered pot over high heat. Add the kale, leeks, and potatoes. Cover, lower the heat to medium, and boil for 20 minutes, stirring occasionally, until the potatoes are tender. Drain well. Return the cooked kale, leeks, and potatoes to the pot. Add the butter or margarine, olive oil, salt, and pepper. Mash the ingredients together, using a potato masher and combining well. Taste for seasoning.

Veggie Burgers

MAKES ABOUT 6 BURGERS

We have been making veggie burgers at **Claire's** for many years, and we are always interested in ways to improve them. These "meaty" burgers are much in demand. Doug Gavoli, a fine cook and a great eater who has been on our staff since 1990, recently added bulgur to the recipe, and it contributes a wonderful texture and flavor. Serve the burgers with mashed potatoes, sautéed spinach, and a salad for dinner, or in a sandwich for lunch. Make the sandwich with good bread, lettuce, sliced tomato and onion, and ketchup and you'll have a nutrient-packed treat.

  ½ cup bulgur (found in health-food stores and some supermarkets)
  1 small yellow onion, finely chopped
  1 medium carrot, minced
  ½ cup finely chopped mushrooms
  3 tablespoons olive oil, plus 1 tablespoon for brushing the burgers
  2 cups rolled oats
1½ cups plain bread crumbs
  ½ cup finely chopped walnuts
  ½ teaspoon dried thyme
  ¼ teaspoon dried sage
    Salt and black pepper to taste
  3 tablespoons water

Preheat the oven to 350 degrees. Put the bulgur in a bowl. Pour boiling water over to just cover the bulgur and set aside.

Heat 3 tablespoons of the olive oil in a nonstick skillet over medium-low heat. Add the chopped vegetables and sauté for 5 minutes, stirring frequently. Add the vegetables to the soaking bulgur and mix well. Add the rolled oats, bread crumbs, walnuts, thyme, sage, salt and pepper, and water. Stir well. Taste for seasoning. Scoop a little burger mixture into your hand and squeeze. If the mixture does not hold together, continue adding water, 1 tablespoon at a time, mixing well after each addition, until it holds together.

Form about 6 balls and flatten them into burger shape. Oil your hands lightly to make the job less messy. Arrange the burgers on a cookie sheet lined with parchment paper. Brush a little oil on each burger, then gently turn the burger and brush the other side. Bake for 10 minutes, then carefully turn each burger to bake the other side for 10 minutes.

Soft Polenta Marinara

SERVES 4

Polenta is often described as a Northern Italian cornmeal mush, but in our family and at **Claire's,** we think of it as a thick stew. Soft polenta topped with a garlicky marinara sauce is one of my favorite meals. At **Claire's,** we often serve it along with roasted eggplant, a tossed salad, and good bread. My mom and many of my aunts serve polenta with a topping of kidney beans, garlic, and parsley, which is delicious and even more nutritious. My grandmother often served us leftover polenta, lightly fried in butter and with Romano on top, for breakfast.

> 9 cups water
> ½ teaspoon salt
> ½ teaspoon black pepper
> 2 tablespoons chopped fresh basil
> 2 tablespoons chopped flat-leaf parsley
> 2 cups yellow cornmeal
> 2 cups warmed Marinara Sauce (see page 127)
> Grated Romano (optional)

Bring the water to a boil in a large covered pot over high heat. Stir in the salt, pepper, basil, and parsley. Slowly add the cornmeal in a stream, stirring constantly. Reduce the heat to low and continue cooking, uncovered, at a low boil, stirring constantly, about 15 minutes. (Wear oven mitts while stirring the polenta, because the boiling cornmeal can bubble onto your hand and burn you.) Pour into a serving bowl and spoon Marinara Sauce on top. Serve with additional Marinara Sauce and grated Romano if desired.

Vegetable and Rice Patties

SERVES 4

We love these little patties served with ketchup, Marinara Sauce (see page 127) or gravy, roasted potatoes, and peas. I guess patties are vegetarian comfort food.

    3 tablespoons olive oil
    2 medium carrots, finely chopped
    1 small yellow onion, minced
    ½ red bell pepper, seeded and minced
    1 rib celery, finely chopped
    1 clove garlic, minced
    ¼ cup finely chopped mushrooms
    1 cup finely chopped fresh spinach
    ¼ teaspoon dried sage
    ½ teaspoon dried thyme
    ¼ cup finely chopped walnuts
    4 cups cooked short-grain brown rice
    1 cup bread crumbs
    3 tablespoons chopped flat-leaf parsley
      Salt and black pepper to taste
    2 eggs, lightly beaten
    2 or 3 tablespoons olive oil for coating the patties

Preheat the oven to 350 degrees. Heat the oil in a skillet over low heat. Add the carrots, onion, bell pepper, celery, and garlic. Cover and cook for 15 minutes, until softened. Stir in the mushrooms, spinach, sage, thyme, and walnuts. Cover and continue cooking for 3 minutes, stirring frequently, until the spinach is wilted. Remove from the heat and turn into a bowl. Add the rice, bread crumbs, parsley, salt, pepper, and eggs. Mix well. Taste for seasoning.

Brush a nonstick cookie sheet with a little olive oil. Form the mixture into patties, using a ½-cup measure for each. Set the patties on the lightly oiled cookie sheet as you form them, and gently turn each over to coat the other side with oil. Bake for 15 to 20 minutes, until lightly browned, then gently turn the patties to bake the other side. Serve with ketchup, Marinara Sauce, or mushroom gravy.

Deep-Dish Gourmet Pizza

SERVES 4

This pizza is actually a savory batter bread, baked with vegetables, cheese, and Marinara Sauce. It's wonderfully aromatic. You can prepare the batter up to a day in advance. At **Claire's** we sometimes bake a layer of ricotta or mascarpone in the middle of this delicious pizza.

    2 cups flour
    1 tablespoon baking powder
    2 tablespoons grated Parmesan
    ½ teaspoon dried oregano
    ¼ cup chopped fresh basil leaves
    2 tablespoons chopped flat-leaf parsley
       Salt and black pepper to taste
    3 eggs
    ⅔ cup milk
    ¼ cup olive oil
    1 cup Marinara Sauce (see page 127)
    2 cups sautéed mixed vegetables of your choice
    4 ounces shredded fontina or mozzarella

Preheat the oven to 375 degrees. In a large bowl, whisk together the flour, baking powder, Parmesan, oregano, basil, parsley, salt, and pepper. In a separate bowl, whisk together the eggs, milk, and olive oil. Pour the liquid ingredients over the dry, all at once, then stir to mix.

Spray an 8-inch square baking pan with nonstick cooking spray. Spoon the batter into the prepared pan, using a rubber spatula to scrape the bowl and smooth the batter. Spoon the Marinara Sauce evenly over the batter. Bake for 35 minutes. Remove from the oven and spoon the sautéed vegetables evenly over the top of the pizza. Sprinkle the fontina or mozzarella evenly over the top. Return to the oven and continue baking about 10 minutes, or until a cake tester inserted in the center comes out nearly dry. Cut into serving pieces. Serve with additional Marinara Sauce if desired.

Desserts

Nothing says home-cooked more beautifully than a freshly baked dessert. And nothing brings more smiles at **Claire's** than our delicious sweets. Our gorgeous selection (twelve to fifteen different cakes, pies, cobblers, crisps, and brownies) is usually the first thing our customers notice.

Our desserts are wildly popular, from simple banana bread and gingerbread to our famous Lithuanian Coffee Cake. We make very basic desserts, the ones our mothers and grandmothers made for us, using high-quality, fresh ingredients, pure vanilla extract, unbleached white and whole-wheat flours, and fresh, seasonal fruits.

Gifts of food are always greatly appreciated. Our customers buy and give our muffin-filled tins and baskets year-round. You might want to surprise a friend with a homemade cake, a pie, or a blueberry buckle. You can present the dessert on a pretty cake dish or in a special tin or basket, wrapped in clear cellophane and tied with colorful ribbons. Most of these recipes are easy to prepare; you can produce delicious and thoughtful gifts in less time than it takes to shop for and buy most presents.

Please remember a few basics when baking. Always read your recipe through before beginning to measure. This will ensure that you have the necessary ingredients and help you follow the steps. When measuring dry ingredients, always level them in the measuring spoon or cup with a rubber spatula or butter knife. I've seen many cooks and bakers measure rounded or heaping spoonfuls of ingredients, but unless a recipe specifies "rounded" or "heaping," you must assume it means a level amount. Accuracy is especially important for proper rising.

You can also help your cakes rise properly by closing the oven door gently; slamming the door can cause a cake to drop in the center. Always wait until your cake is cooled to room temperature before you frost or glaze it, or the topping will melt.

Here's to wonderful desserts!

Lithuanian Coffee Cake

SERVES 10 TO 12

This is our most popular cake at **Claire's**. After eighteen years, it is still the splurge of choice for many. We have changed the recipe over the years, switching to low-fat sour cream, but it is still very rich and incredibly delicious.

Filling:

¼ cup packed dark brown sugar
2 tablespoons granulated sugar
1 teaspoon cinnamon
1 tablespoon ground coffee (not brewed)
¼ cup chopped walnuts
¼ cup raisins

Cake:

8 tablespoons (1 stick) butter, softened to room temperature
1 cup granulated sugar
2 eggs
1 tablespoon brewed coffee, chilled
1 teaspoon vanilla extract
1 cup low-fat sour cream
2 cups unbleached flour
1 teaspoon baking soda
1 teaspoon baking powder

Prepare the filling by combining the filling ingredients in a small bowl. Stir to combine well. Set aside. Preheat the oven to 350 degrees.

For the cake, cream the butter and sugar in a mixing bowl, using a hand mixer on medium speed for 45 seconds. Scrape down the sides with a rubber spatula. Add the eggs and beat for 30 seconds. Scrape down the sides of the bowl. Add the coffee, vanilla extract, and sour cream. Beat on low speed for 30 seconds, until well creamed. Scrape down the sides of the bowl.

In a separate mixing bowl, sift together the flour, baking soda, and baking

powder. Pour the creamed mixture over the top of the flour mixture, scraping the bowl well. Mix on low speed for 45 seconds just to combine, stopping to scrape down the sides of the bowl.

Prepare a 10-cup bundt pan, either by thoroughly spraying with nonstick cooking spray or greasing with shortening and flouring the pan. Pour in half the batter. Sprinkle half the filling evenly over the top of the batter. Pour the remaining batter evenly over the filling. Use a rubber spatula to scrape the batter from the bowl and smooth the batter. Sprinkle the remaining filling evenly over the batter.

Bake in the center of the oven for 50 to 55 minutes, until a cake tester inserted in the center comes out clean. Remove the cake from the oven and let it cool in the pan for 5 minutes; then turn it out onto a plate. Serve warm or cooled to room temperature, drizzled with a glaze, frosted with Buttercream Frosting (see page 257), or sprinkled with powdered sugar.

Carrot Cake

SERVES 8

I remember my surprise when my Aunt Jerry, one of the best bakers I know, served a carrot cake to our family many years ago. Although my aunt's culinary talents were well known, I wasn't so sure I wanted a vegetable in my dessert. What a delicious revelation! Each day at **Claire's** we bake a number of moist carrot cakes packed with pineapple and walnuts.

1½ cups unbleached flour
1½ cups sugar
 1 teaspoon salt
 2 teaspoons baking soda
 2 teaspoons cinnamon
½ teaspoon ground nutmeg
 3 eggs
¾ cup soybean or vegetable oil
 1 cup drained crushed pineapple
¾ cup grated carrots
¾ cup chopped walnuts
⅓ cup raisins

Preheat the oven to 350 degrees. In a large bowl, whisk together the flour, sugar, salt, baking soda, cinnamon, and nutmeg. In a separate bowl, beat the eggs for 1 minute, using a hand mixer. Add the oil and mix on medium speed for 1 minute. Stir in the drained pineapple. Pour this mixture all at once over the dry ingredients and mix lightly to combine. Stir in the carrots, walnuts, and raisins. Mix just to combine, using a spoon.

Prepare a 10-cup bundt pan with nonstick cooking spray, or grease and flour the pan. Pour the batter into the prepared pan. Bake on the center rack of the oven about 1 hour and 10 minutes, or until a cake tester inserted in the center comes out clean. Remove from the oven and let stand for 5 minutes; then turn out and cool to room temperature before frosting with Buttercream Frosting (see page 257).

Chocolate Cake

SERVES 8

This cake is wonderful and a big success any way we present it at **Claire's.** We serve it plain, or with our Buttercream Frosting (see page 257), or we spoon peanut butter or raspberry preserves over the top of the batter just before baking. Or we slice a fresh banana and push the slices into the batter before baking. We use about twenty quarts of this batter every day and it has only gotten more popular over the past eighteen years.

    8 tablespoons (1 stick) butter, at room temperature
1½ cups sugar
    3 eggs
1⅛ teaspoons vanilla extract
    2 cups flour
    ¾ cup unsweetened cocoa powder
    ½ teaspoon salt
1⅛ teaspoons baking soda
1⅛ teaspoons baking powder
1½ cups buttermilk or sour milk

Preheat the oven to 350 degrees. Cream the butter in a mixing bowl, using a hand mixer. Add the sugar and beat on medium speed, scraping the sides of the bowl as needed, until well blended, about 1 minute. Add the eggs and vanilla extract and continue to beat on medium speed about 30 seconds, until well blended.

In a separate large bowl, sift together the flour, cocoa powder, salt, baking soda, and baking powder. Spoon all of the creamed butter mixture onto the sifted dry ingredients. Pour the buttermilk over the top. Mix, using a hand mixer on low speed, about 1 minute, scraping down the sides of the bowl 2 or 3 times.

Spray a 10-cup bundt pan with nonstick cooking spray, or grease and flour the pan. Spoon the batter into the prepared pan, scraping the sides of the bowl. Smooth the batter. Bake in the center of the oven about 50 minutes, or until a cake tester inserted in the center comes out clean. Remove from the oven and let stand for 5 minutes, then invert onto a cake dish.

Banana Bread

MAKES A 9-x-5-INCH LOAF

Banana bread is one of the four basic batters we make each day at **Claire's.** We offer it plain, with walnuts, marbled with chocolate, or baked on a cookie sheet with walnuts and chocolate chips and cut into large squares. We always have bananas on hand, ripening until their skin is just speckled enough for the bananas to be sweet and tender. This bread keeps well for days; the flavor even improves. Just wrap the loaf in foil after it cools and leave it on your counter.

> 2 cups unbleached flour
> 1½ teaspoons baking powder
> ¼ teaspoon baking soda
> ¼ teaspoon salt
> 7 eggs
> 4 tablespoons (½ stick) melted butter or margarine
> ½ cup sugar
> 2 large, ripe bananas, mashed
> ⅓ cup chopped walnuts (optional)

Preheat the oven to 350 degrees. In a large bowl, sift together the flour, baking powder, baking soda, and salt. Set aside. In a separate bowl, whisk the eggs lightly. Whisk in the butter or margarine and sugar, mixing well. Stir in the mashed bananas, combining well. Add the flour mixture to the egg mixture and stir until just mixed. Stir in the walnuts if using.

Spray a 9-x-5-inch loaf pan with nonstick cooking spray. Turn the batter into the prepared pan. Bake for 1¼ hours, or until a cake tester inserted in the center comes out just dry. Remove from the oven and let stand for 5 minutes, then turn out and serve warm or at room temperature.

Pumpkin Bread

MAKES A 9-X-5-INCH LOAF

Pumpkin bread is a perennial at **Claire's.** It is as much a part of fall and winter as the changing colors of the leaves and cool temperatures. We always look forward to the wonderful aromas of our fall specialties, and this pumpkin bread is one of the delicious ways we celebrate the season.

    2 eggs
    1 cup sugar
    ¼ cup soybean or vegetable oil
    1 cup fresh or canned pureed pumpkin
    ¼ cup buttermilk
    2 cups unbleached flour
    2 teaspoons baking powder
    ½ teaspoon salt
    ¼ teaspoon baking soda
    ½ teaspoon ground ginger
    ¼ teaspoon ground cloves
    ¼ teaspoon cinnamon
    ¼ cup chopped walnuts
    ¼ cup golden raisins

Preheat the oven to 375 degrees. Combine the eggs, sugar, oil, pumpkin, and buttermilk in a bowl. Beat to mix well, using a hand mixer or whisk. In a separate bowl, whisk together the flour, baking powder, salt, baking soda, ginger, cloves, and cinnamon. Pour the liquid ingredients over the dry all at once and mix with a spoon just to combine. Don't beat the batter or you will have a tough bread. Gently stir in the walnuts and raisins.

Spray a 9-x-5-inch loaf pan with nonstick cooking spray, or grease and flour the pan. Pour the batter into the pan. Bake on the center rack of the oven about 1¼ hours, or until a cake tester inserted in the center comes out clean. Remove from the oven and let stand for 5 minutes. Turn the bread out of the pan to cool. This bread is delicious alone or spread with plain yogurt or low-fat cream cheese. Wrap any remaining bread in foil to store for up to 3 days.

Sugar-Free Blueberry Cake

SERVES 8

This cake has brought special pleasure to our customers who don't eat sugar, although we all love it. The apple and orange juices, along with the blueberries, provide a natural, healthful sweetness.

>   3 eggs
>   8 tablespoons (1 stick) butter, margarine, or soy margarine, at room temperature (soy margarine can be found in most health-food stores)
>   ⅓ cup orange juice (freshly squeezed is best)
>   ⅓ cup apple cider
>   ⅓ cup milk
>   ½ teaspoon vanilla extract
> 2½ cups unbleached flour
>   1 teaspoon baking soda
>   2 teaspoons baking powder
>   1 teaspoon cinnamon
>   1 teaspoon freshly grated orange zest
>   ½ cup chopped walnuts
>   ¾ cup fresh blueberries

Preheat the oven to 350 degrees. In a large bowl, beat together the eggs, butter or margarine, orange juice, cider, milk, and vanilla extract about 1½ minutes, using a hand mixer on medium speed. Scrape down the sides of the bowl with a rubber spatula 2 or 3 times during the mixing.

In a separate bowl, whisk together the flour, baking soda, baking powder, cinnamon, and orange zest. Add the dry mixture to the liquid mixture all at once. Mix just to combine, using a hand mixer on medium speed. Stir in the walnuts and blueberries.

Spray a 10-cup bundt pan with nonstick cooking spray, or grease and flour the pan. Pour the batter into the prepared pan, using a rubber spatula to scrape the bowl. Smooth the top. Bake in the center of the oven about 50 minutes, or until a cake tester inserted in the center comes out clean. Remove from the oven and let stand for 5 minutes before inverting onto a cake dish.

Dairy-Free Chocolate-Raspberry Cake

SERVES 10 TO 12

This cake is so rich and moist that it's hard to believe it's also lactose- and cholesterol-free and low in fat.

2¼ cups unbleached flour
1 teaspoon baking soda
¼ teaspoon salt
½ cup unsweetened cocoa powder
½ cup packed dark brown sugar
¼ cup unsweetened applesauce
¼ cup soybean or vegetable oil
¾ cup cold water
1 cup honey
1 tablespoon cider vinegar
1 tablespoon vanilla extract
½ cup raspberry preserves

Preheat the oven to 350 degrees. In a large bowl, sift together the flour, baking soda, salt, and cocoa powder. Mix in the brown sugar. In a separate bowl, whisk together the applesauce, oil, water, honey, vinegar, and vanilla extract. Mix until well blended. Pour the liquid over the dry mixture all at once. Beat with a spoon until smooth.

Prepare a 10-cup bundt pan either by spraying with nonstick cooking spray or greasing with shortening and dusting with flour. Pour the batter into the prepared pan and smooth the top. Spoon the preserves evenly over the top of the batter. Bake in the center of the oven for 40 to 50 minutes, until a cake tester inserted in the center comes out clean. Remove the cake from the oven, let stand for 5 minutes, then turn out onto a large plate. (Be careful: hot preserves will trickle down the cake and can burn you.) Serve warm or at room temperature. This cake keeps well for 3 to 4 days wrapped in foil.

Cranberry-Walnut Bread

MAKES A 9-X-5-INCH LOAF

This bread is a fall favorite at **Claire's.** You'll enjoy it anytime—for breakfast, brunch, your afternoon coffee break, or evening dessert. It's lovely plain or spread with a little low-fat cream cheese.

3 cups unbleached flour
1 teaspoon baking soda
1 teaspoon baking powder
1 teaspoon salt
2 eggs
1 cup sugar
4 tablespoons (½ stick) butter, margarine, or soy margarine, melted (soy margarine can be found in most health-food stores)
1¼ cups buttermilk or sour milk
3 tablespoons freshly grated orange zest
1 tablespoon freshly squeezed orange juice
1¼ cup fresh cranberries
¾ cup chopped walnuts

Preheat the oven to 350 degrees. In a large bowl, sift together the flour, baking soda, baking powder, and salt. In a separate bowl, whisk the eggs for 30 seconds. Add the sugar, melted butter or margarine, buttermilk or sour milk, orange zest, and juice. Beat for 1 minute, until smooth, with a whisk. Pour over the flour mixture all at once and mix with a spoon to combine well. Stir in the cranberries and walnuts; do not beat.

Spray a 9-x-5-inch loaf pan with nonstick cooking spray, or grease and flour the pan. Pour the batter into the prepared pan. Bake on the center rack of the oven about 1½ hours, until a cake tester inserted in the center comes out clean. Remove from the oven and let stand for 5 minutes before turning out to cool.

Lemon Poppyseed Cake

MAKES AN 8-INCH SQUARE CAKE

This cake rises beautifully, and its wonderful aroma will fill your kitchen. Serve it plain with just a dusting of confectioners' sugar with afternoon coffee or tea, or frost it with Buttercream Frosting (see page 257) mixed with a little freshly grated lemon zest for an impressive dessert. During the holidays, we bake little loaves of this cake, top them with a thick lemon glaze, and wrap each in clear cellophane after the glaze has set, tying them with colorful ribbons for gifts.

1¾ cups flour
⅔ cup sugar
1 tablespoon freshly grated lemon zest
1½ teaspoons baking powder
2 teaspoons poppyseeds
1 egg
¾ cup milk
¼ cup soybean or vegetable oil
1 tablespoon fresh lemon juice

Preheat the oven to 375 degrees. In a large bowl, whisk together the flour, sugar, lemon zest, baking powder, and poppyseeds. In a separate bowl, whisk together the egg, milk, oil, and lemon juice about 30 seconds. Add this to the dry ingredients all at once and stir until well combined.

Spray an 8-inch square pan with nonstick cooking spray, or grease and flour the pan. Pour the batter into the prepared pan, scraping the bowl with a rubber spatula. Smooth the top. Bake in the center of the oven about 45 minutes, or until a cake tester inserted into the center comes out clean. Remove from the oven and let stand for 5 minutes before inverting onto a cake plate.

Pumpkin-Walnut Pie

MAKES A 9-INCH PIE

Everyone loves this Grand Marnier–flavored pumpkin pie.

    1 cup chopped walnuts
    1 cup packed dark brown sugar
  1½ teaspoons cinnamon
    3 eggs
    1 cup evaporated milk
    ¼ teaspoon salt
    ½ teaspoon ground ginger
    ⅛ teaspoon ground cloves
    1 pinch ground nutmeg
    1 cup pumpkin puree, canned or fresh
    2 tablespoons Grand Marnier liqueur
  One 9-inch unbaked pie crust (store-bought is fine)

Preheat the oven to 375 degrees. In a small bowl, combine the walnuts, ¼ cup of the brown sugar, and ½ teaspoon of the cinnamon. Spread evenly on the bottom of the pie crust. In a separate bowl, whisk the eggs about 30 seconds. Add the evaporated milk, the remaining 1 teaspoon cinnamon, salt, ginger, cloves, nutmeg, the remaining ¾ cup brown sugar, pumpkin, and Grand Marnier. Whisk about 30 seconds, until smooth. Pour over the walnuts in the pie crust.

Bake on a cookie sheet for 40 to 45 minutes, until the center is set. Remove from the oven and let stand for 15 minutes before serving.

Sweet Potato Pie

MAKES A 9-INCH PIE

I ate my first sweet potato pie back in 1975. It was love at first sight, smell, and taste. A favorite customer named Bob brought me a piece of his mother's famous pie along with a sketchy recipe. The pie was marvelous, and I can only hope mine is nearly as good.

    1¼ cups mashed cooked sweet potatoes (about 2 large potatoes)
     2 eggs, lightly beaten
     ½ cup packed dark brown sugar
     2 tablespoons dark molasses
     1 cup evaporated skimmed milk
     1 teaspoon cinnamon
        Pinch ground nutmeg
     ⅛ teaspoon ground cloves
    One 9-inch prebaked pie crust (store-bought is fine)

Preheat the oven to 375 degrees. In a bowl, combine all the ingredients except the pie crust. Whisk well to blend, about 1 minute. Pour the filling into the baked crust.

Bake on a cookie sheet for 35 to 40 minutes, until the center is set. Remove from the oven and allow to cool for 15 minutes before serving.

Texas Walnut Pie

MAKES A 9-INCH PIE

This dessert is addictive. As if the ingredients weren't rich enough, some of us eat this wonderful pie with whipped cream on top! Although everyone loves it, we make this sinfully luscious dessert infrequently.

    4 eggs
    ¼ teaspoon salt
    1 cup sugar
 1⅓ cups light corn syrup
    4 tablespoons (½ stick) butter, melted
    1 teaspoon vanilla extract
    1 cup walnut halves
One 9-inch prebaked pie crust (store-bought is fine)

Preheat the oven to 400 degrees. In a bowl, combine the eggs, salt, and sugar. Whisk well. Add the corn syrup, melted butter, and vanilla extract. Whisk well. Spread the walnuts evenly on the bottom of the baked pie crust. Pour the filling over the walnuts.

Bake on a cookie sheet for 15 minutes, then lower the heat to 350 degrees and bake for another 30 to 35 minutes, until the center is just set. Let stand for 15 minutes before serving.

Ricotta Pie

MAKES A 9-INCH PIE

This is our traditional holiday pie at my mom's house, and the whole family loves it. We serve it year-round at **Claire's,** and it's delicious whether eaten while still warm or chilled. It needs only a sprinkle of confectioners' sugar on top.

     1 pound ricotta
     2 eggs, lightly beaten
     ¼ cup sugar
     2 tablespoons unbleached flour
     1 tablespoon freshly grated lemon zest
       Juice of ½ lemon
     ¼ teaspoon vanilla extract
     3 tablespoons heavy cream or milk
    One 9-inch prebaked pie crust (store-bought is fine)

Preheat the oven to 375 degrees. In a bowl, combine the ricotta, eggs, sugar, flour, lemon zest, lemon juice, vanilla extract, and cream or milk. Beat well with a spoon. Pour the filling into the baked pie crust. Smooth the top with a rubber spatula.

Set the pie on a cookie sheet and bake on the center shelf of the oven for 40 to 45 minutes, until the center is just set and the pie is golden brown. Let stand for 15 minutes before serving.

Apple-Crumb Pie

MAKES A 9-INCH PIE

There may be little to add to what's already been said in praise of apple-crumb pie, but we can never make too many of these beauties at **Claire's.** As quickly as we can peel the apples and bake the pies, that's how quickly they sell. Apple pie is surely one of our national treasures. Bake one for your family or friends as soon as the autumn McIntosh, Rome, or Cortland apples are available.

    8 apples, cored, peeled, and sliced ¼ inch thick (about 8 cups)
      Juice of 1 lemon
    ¾ cup packed dark brown sugar
    1 teaspoon cinnamon
    ½ teaspoon ground nutmeg
  One 9-inch unbaked pie crust (store-bought is fine)

Crumb topping:

    ½ cup packed dark brown sugar
    ½ cup unbleached flour
    ¼ cup rolled oats
    ½ teaspoon cinnamon
    4 tablespoons (½ stick) butter, at room temperature

Preheat the oven to 375 degrees. Combine the apples and lemon juice in a bowl, tossing to coat well. Add the brown sugar, cinnamon, and nutmeg and toss again to coat well.

Prepare the topping: in a bowl, combine the brown sugar, flour, oats, and cinnamon, tossing well. Add the butter and work in, using your fingers, until the mixture resembles coarse crumbs.

Lift the apples out of the bowl and mound them in the pie crust, using your hands so that most of the liquid remains in the bowl. Sprinkle the topping evenly over the apples.

Bake the pie, centered in the oven on a cookie sheet, about 1 hour, until the crumbs are browned and the apples are tender when tested with a fork. Remove from the oven and let stand for 15 minutes before serving.

Strawberry Bread

MAKES A 9-X-5-INCH LOAF

This delicious light bread is perfect to enjoy after a meal on a hot summer day. Serve it alone or with frozen yogurt, or toast a slice the next day for breakfast.

    2 eggs
    1 cup sugar
    ⅓ cup soybean or vegetable oil
    ⅓ cup unsweetened applesauce
    1½ cups unbleached flour
    1 teaspoon cinnamon
    ½ teaspoon baking soda
    ½ teaspoon salt
    1 tablespoon freshly grated lemon zest
    1½ cups sliced fresh strawberries
    ½ cup chopped walnuts

Preheat the oven to 350 degrees. Lightly whisk the eggs in a mixing bowl. Add the sugar, oil, and applesauce, beating for 1 minute. In a separate bowl, whisk together the flour, cinnamon, baking soda, salt, and lemon zest. Pour the liquid ingredients over this mixture all at once and stir well to combine. Stir in the strawberries and walnuts.

Spray a 9-x-5-inch loaf pan with nonstick cooking spray, or grease and flour the pan. Pour the batter into the prepared pan, using a rubber spatula to scrape the bowl. Smooth the top. Bake in the center of the oven about 1½ hours, until a cake tester inserted in the center comes out clean. Let stand for 5 minutes before inverting onto a cake dish. Carefully turn so that the flat side is on the bottom.

Pear and Apple Cobbler

SERVES 8

We use Cortland or Rome apples and ripe yellow-green pears for this delicious and nutritious dessert. Leftovers are wonderful for breakfast, topped with non-fat yogurt and a little wheat germ.

  6 apples, cored and cut into eighths
    Juice of 1 lemon
  6 pears, cored and cut into eighths
  ¼ cup packed dark brown sugar
  1 teaspoon vanilla extract
  1 teaspoon cinnamon

Topping:

  1½ cups rolled oats
  1½ cups whole-wheat flour
    1 cup granulated sugar
    1 tablespoon baking powder
  ¼ teaspoon cinnamon
  ¼ cup unsweetened applesauce
    4 tablespoons (½ stick) butter, margarine, or soy margarine, melted (soy
        margarine can be found in most health-food stores)
    1 cup low-fat milk

Preheat the oven to 350 degrees. In a large bowl, combine the apples, lemon juice, pears, brown sugar, vanilla extract, and cinnamon. Toss well. Turn into a rectangular glass baking dish.

Prepare the topping: in a bowl, combine the oats, flour, sugar, baking powder, cinnamon, applesauce, melted butter or margarine, and milk. Mix well with a spoon.

Drop spoonfuls of the topping evenly on the fruit mixture. Bake for 1½ hours, or until the fruit is softened to your liking and the topping is golden brown. Serve hot or at room temperature.

Indian Pudding

SERVES 8 TO 10

My good friend Claudia is a marvelous baker and a thoughtful person, the kind of friend who will surprise you with homemade peanut butter bread waiting for you in your mailbox along with the day's mail. Claudia once brought an antique crock filled with her grandmother's Indian pudding over to our house. The crock was beautiful, but the real treasure was inside. This pudding, served warm with vanilla ice cream or whipped cream on top, is the perfect dessert for a cold winter night.

  6 cups milk
½ cup yellow cornmeal
  3 eggs
  1 teaspoon salt
½ teaspoon ground ginger
½ teaspoon ground nutmeg
  3 tablespoons butter
1⅓ cups molasses
⅔ cup golden raisins

Preheat the oven to 300 degrees. Scald the milk in a saucepan over medium heat. Slowly add the cornmeal in a steady stream, whisking continuously. Raise the heat to high and continue whisking until the mixture comes to a boil. Reduce the heat to low and cook for 15 minutes, whisking constantly, until the mixture is thickened and creamy.

In a large bowl, whisk the eggs for 30 seconds. Slowly add the cornmeal mixture to the beaten eggs, whisking constantly. Add the salt, ginger, nutmeg, butter, molasses, and raisins. Stir to melt the butter and thoroughly mix the ingredients.

Pour into an oiled crock or glass baking dish. Cover and bake about 2 hours, until set.

Oatmeal-Raisin Cookies

MAKES ABOUT 3 DOZEN COOKIES

These were the quintessential after-school treat for many of us during our childhood. Our customers still love them for a work or study break treat. And yes, they're still perfect for dunking in a glass of milk.

1¾ cups unbleached flour
1 teaspoon baking powder
1 teaspoon baking soda
1 teaspoon salt
1 teaspoon cinnamon
½ teaspoon ground nutmeg
2 eggs
1 cup vegetable shortening
1½ cups packed dark brown sugar
1 teaspoon vanilla extract
½ cup milk
3 cups rolled oats
1 cup raisins
½ cup chopped walnuts (optional)

Preheat the oven to 350 degrees. Line 3 cookie sheets with parchment paper or spray with nonstick cooking spray. In a large bowl, combine the flour, baking powder, baking soda, salt, cinnamon, and nutmeg. In a separate bowl, beat the eggs for 30 seconds, using a hand mixer on medium speed. Add the shortening and brown sugar and beat for 2 minutes on medium speed, until well mixed. Add the vanilla extract and milk. Beat for 1 minute on low speed, until blended. Pour the wet mixture all at once over the flour mixture, and mix well with a spoon. Stir in the oats, then stir in the raisins and walnuts, if using.

Drop heaping tablespoons of the batter onto the prepared cookie sheets, leaving space in between for spreading. You should fit 12 cookies on each sheet. Bake in the center of the oven for 15 to 20 minutes, until golden brown. Let stand for 15 minutes before removing from the cookie sheets.

Brownies

MAKES AN 8-INCH SQUARE PAN OF BROWNIES

These are the best brownies, the chewiest and richest, a chocolate lover's jackpot.

    3 ounces semisweet chocolate, chopped
    8 tablespoons (1 stick) butter, at room temperature
    ¾ cup unbleached flour
    ¼ teaspoon baking powder
    ¼ teaspoon salt
    2 eggs
    1 cup sugar
    1 teaspoon vanilla extract

Preheat the oven to 350 degrees. Combine the chocolate and butter in the top of a double boiler and set over gently boiling water. Stir frequently until the chocolate and butter melt. Meanwhile, in a large bowl, combine the flour, baking powder, and salt. In a separate bowl, beat together the eggs, sugar, and vanilla extract, using a hand mixer on medium speed, for about 2 minutes. When the chocolate and butter have melted, add to the beaten eggs, sugar, and vanilla extract, whisking well. Pour this over the flour mixture and whisk together until all the flour is mixed in.

Spray an 8-inch square pan with nonstick cooking spray, or grease and flour the pan. Turn the batter into the prepared pan, using a rubber spatula to scrape the bowl. Smooth the top. Bake in the center of the oven about 30 minutes, until a cake tester inserted in the center comes out clean. Let stand for 5 minutes before cutting into squares.

Gingerbread

MAKES AN 8-INCH SQUARE GINGERBREAD

We love gingerbread at **Claire's.** The delightful aroma gets everyone's attention as it fills the restaurant, and eager taste-testers are always available to critique a fresh batch. We serve it plain just as soon as it cools down enough to cut into chunks, or with whipped cream mixed with a little lemon zest, and it's wonderful served warm with fresh lemon pudding on top.

1 cup sugar
1 cup molasses
1 cup soybean or vegetable oil
3 eggs
½ teaspoon salt
1 teaspoon ground ginger
1 teaspoon cinnamon
2 cups flour
2 teaspoons baking soda
1 cup boiling water

Preheat the oven to 350 degrees. In a large bowl, whisk together the sugar, molasses, oil, and eggs, beating until smooth. In a separate bowl with a dry whisk, combine the salt, ginger, cinnamon, flour, and baking soda. Turn the dry ingredients into wet ingredients and whisk together for 30 seconds. Add the boiling water and whisk about 1 minute, until smooth. You should have a thin batter.

Spray an 8-inch square pan with nonstick cooking spray, or grease and flour the pan. Pour the batter into the pan, scraping the bowl. Bake in the center of the oven about 1 hour, or until a cake tester inserted in the center comes out clean. Let stand for 5 minutes before inverting onto a cake plate.

Blueberry Buckle

SERVES 8

Summers would not be complete without this beautiful blueberry buckle, just bursting with plump berries. If you're lucky enough to pass a roadside farm stand selling fresh blueberries, stop and get a basket for this delicious dessert.

¼ cup vegetable shortening
⅔ cup sugar
1 egg
½ cup milk
2 cups unbleached flour
½ teaspoon salt
2 teaspoons baking powder
1 tablespoon freshly grated lemon zest
2 cups fresh blueberries

Topping:

½ cup packed dark brown sugar
½ cup unbleached flour
1 teaspoon cinnamon
1 tablespoon freshly grated lemon zest
4 tablespoons (½ stick) butter, at room temperature
½ cup chopped walnuts

Preheat the oven to 350 degrees. In a large bowl, cream the shortening with a hand mixer on medium speed for 1 minute. Add the sugar and continue beating about 1 minute. Add the egg and continue beating for 1 minute. Add the milk and continue beating for 1 minute, using a rubber spatula to scrape the sides of the bowl as needed.

In a separate bowl, whisk together the flour, salt, baking powder, and lemon zest. Add this mixture to the creamed mixture. Beat with a hand mixer on medium speed about 2 minutes, until combined, scraping the sides of the bowl as needed. Gently stir in the blueberries.

Prepare the topping in a separate bowl. Combine the brown sugar, flour, cinnamon, and lemon zest. Add the butter and rub the mixture together with your fingers until it resembles coarse meal. Add the walnuts and toss.

Spray an 8-inch square pan with nonstick cooking spray, or grease and flour the pan. Pour the batter into the prepared pan. Smooth the top with a rubber spatula. Sprinkle the topping evenly over the top of the batter. Bake in the center of the oven about 1 hour and 10 minutes, or until a cake tester inserted in the center comes out clean. Let stand for 5 minutes, then cut into squares.

Applesauce-Spice Cake

MAKES AN 8-INCH SQUARE CAKE

This cake is a fall favorite at **Claire's.** Serve it alone or topped with a little plain or vanilla-flavored yogurt mixed with some cinnamon.

  1¾ cups unbleached flour
  1 teaspoon baking soda
  ½ teaspoon salt
  1½ teaspoons cinnamon
  ½ teaspoon ground nutmeg
  ¼ teaspoon ground cloves
  4 tablespoons (½ stick) butter, margarine, or soy margarine, at room
      temperature (soy margarine can be found in most health-food stores)
  1 cup sugar
  1 egg
  1¼ cups unsweetened applesauce
  ½ cup golden raisins
  ½ cup chopped walnuts

Preheat the oven to 350 degrees. Combine the flour, baking soda, salt, cinnamon, nutmeg, and cloves in a bowl. In a separate large bowl, cream the butter or margarine with the sugar until light and fluffy, about 2 minutes, using a hand mixer on medium speed. Add the egg and applesauce and continue beating for 1 minute, using a rubber spatula to scrape down the sides as needed. Add the flour mixture and beat about 2 minutes to combine. Stir in the raisins and walnuts.

Spray an 8-inch square pan with nonstick cooking spray, or grease and flour the pan. Turn the batter into the prepared pan, using a rubber spatula to scrape the bowl. Smooth the top. Bake in the center of the oven for 50 minutes, or until a cake tester inserted in the center comes out clean. Let stand for 5 minutes, then cut into squares.

Buttercream Frosting

MAKES ENOUGH TO FROST A LARGE BUNDT CAKE

This frosting is the fluffy white cream that is generously spread on the delicious cakes that have been our trademark at **Claire's** since 1975.

4 tablespoons (½ stick) butter, at room temperature
4 tablespoons (½ stick) margarine or soy margarine, at room temperature
   (soy margarine can be found at most health-food stores)
2 cups confectioners' sugar, sifted
1 teaspoon vanilla extract

Using a hand mixer on medium speed, beat together the butter and margarine about 3 minutes, or until light and creamy. Scrape down the sides of the bowl with a rubber spatula as needed. Add the confectioners' sugar, ½ cup at a time, beating about 2 minutes after each addition, until light and creamy. Beat in the vanilla extract.

INDEX